Pearson

Y0-BSM-153

Dramatized Bible Readings

Dramatized Bible Readings

Miriam B. Maddox

BAKER BOOK HOUSE

Grand Rapids, Michigan 49506

With deep appreciation
I dedicate this book
to
Audrey, Bill, and Tim
for their
love and encouragement
to me.

Copyright 1980 by
Baker Book House Company

ISBN: 0-8010-6106-7

Printed in the United States of America

Acknowledgments

I thank the Lord for His Word and the many ways He uses it to speak to me. This has been especially true as I have prepared these readings.

I am also grateful to:

Dr. James Phipps for the persistent interest he has shown in getting these readings published;

Dr. Robert Gromacki who has given freely of his time and guidance in sharing with me his skill and expertise;

Pastor Lawrence G. Fetzer for his help in choosing the most descriptive passages of Scripture;

Mrs. Irene Gidley for her typing ability.

Preface

In over twenty years of teaching speech, I found adequate material available in the areas of Fundamentals of Speech, Debate, Oral Interpretation, Play Production, Dramatic Art, and Speech Therapy. However, there was a void in material available for my class in Advanced Oral Interpretation.

The idea came to me that something stimulating could be produced by reading aloud dramatic portions of the Bible. Thus the dramatized Bible readings were developed.

The purpose of the dramatized Bible readings is to create for the audience the opportunity to experience a living literature—a literature that is emotionally and intellectually invigorating, one that can vitalize the human spirit. This is accomplished by a group of oral interpreters reading a carefully planned script. Natural responsive voices provide variety and freedom to individualize the characters. Each part should be represented by a different voice. A manuscript is used throughout the program.

Stools, ladders, and benches in a variety of heights creates an unusual setting. The use of spotlights with different colored "gels" helps to guide the audience from one character to another, getting the story through to the audience by sound and light.

Effective costuming can be accomplished by using academic gowns and choir robes.

The scripts are taken directly from the King James Version. Reading the Bible together has been a rewarding experience for both individuals and groups.

Isaiah 55:11 promises: "So shall my word be that goeth forth out of my mouth: it shall not return unto me void, but shall accomplish that which I please."

Miriam B. Maddox

Contents

Production Notes

Staging

Stage curtains, plain backdrops, or screens may be used.
Stools, ladders, and benches in a variety of heights creates an unusual setting and makes it possible for each reader to be heard and seen.

Lighting

The movement of this program depends on the coordination of the lights and voices. The light should come on just before the speaker starts speaking, and fade as he finishes. Several spotlights utilizing different colored "gels" help to guide the audience from one reader to another. Accurate timing of the lights makes the story live. The light cues ( ) are on the regular script. When God or Satan speaks, it is very effective to have the voice come from behind the curtain, while the light shines in front of the curtain to pinpoint the position of the voice. The audience will hear the voice—but will see only the light.

Costumes

Costumes should be simple, such as academic gowns or choir robes (a variety of colors), or plain attire.

Voice

Good projection of tone and clear articulation are essential. Be sure that the voices are distinctive. Work for variety in pitch and tone.

Focus

Each character and narrator should focus his attention on a certain central predetermined point at the back of the room when he is speaking. This will give unity and continuity to the work. When one is not speaking, the head is bowed.

Keep the production moving with quick response to cues.

Develop a free-flowing atmosphere to insure audience participation.

Simplicity is the key to a successful production.

Character study and interpretation in *Dramatized Bible Readings* are as important and more difficult than stage acting.

Dramatized Bible Readings

Part One

The Old Testament

The Temptation; The Wrong Choice

Adam and Eve

Stage Layout*

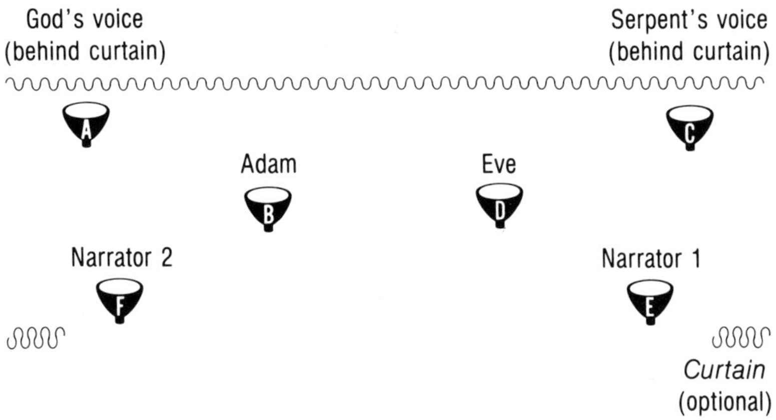

God's voice
(behind curtain)

Serpent's voice
(behind curtain)

A

C

Adam

Eve

B

D

Narrator 2

Narrator 1

F

E

Curtain
(optional)

Production Plots

	Lights	Character	Costume	Props
A	White light	God	—	—
B	Blue light	Adam	Blue robe	24-inch ladder
C	Red light	Serpent	—	—
D	Yellow light	Eve	Yellow robe	24-inch ladder
E	Pink light	Narrator 1	White robe	18-inch stool
F	Pink light	Narrator 2	White robe	18-inch stool

*For Production Notes, see page 9.

Genesis 2-3

Narrator 1

God blessed the seventh day, and sanctified it: and rested from all his work which God created and made.

These are the generations of the heavens and of the earth when they were created, in the day that the Lord God made the earth and the heavens, and every plant of the field before it was in the earth, and every herb in the field before it grew: for the Lord God had not caused it to rain upon the earth, and there was not a man to till the ground. But there went up a mist from the earth, and watered the whole face of the ground.

Narrator 2

And the Lord God formed man of the dust of the ground, and breathed into his nostrils the breath of life; and man became a living soul.

And the Lord God planted a garden eastward in Eden; and there he put the man whom he had formed. And out of the ground made the Lord God to grow every tree that is pleasant to the sight, and good for food; the tree of life also in the midst of the garden, and the tree of knowledge of good and evil. And a river went out of Eden to water the garden;

And the Lord God took the man, and put him into the garden of Eden to dress it, and to keep it. And the Lord God commanded. . .

God

Of every tree of the garden thou mayest freely eat: but of the tree of the knowledge of good and evil, thou shalt not eat of it: for in the day that thou eatest thereof, thou shalt surely die.

It is not good that the man should be alone; I will make him an help meet for him.

Narrator 1

And out of the ground the Lord God formed every beast of the field, and every fowl of the air; and brought them unto Adam to see what he would call them: and whatsoever Adam called every living creature, that was the name thereof.

And the rib, which the Lord God had taken from man, made he a woman, and brought her unto the man.

Adam

This is now bone of my bones, and flesh of my flesh: she shall be called Woman, because she was taken out of Man. Therefore shall a man leave his father and his mother, and shall cleave unto his wife: and they shall be one flesh.

Narrator 2

And they were both naked, the man and his wife, and were not ashamed.

Now the serpent was more subtle than any beast of the field which the Lord God had made. And he said unto the woman . . .

Serpent

Yea, hath God said, Ye shall not eat of every tree of the garden?

Eve

We may eat of the fruit of the trees of the garden: but of the fruit of the tree which is in the midst of the garden, God hath said, Ye shall not eat of it, neither shall ye touch it, lest ye die.

Serpent

Ye shall not surely die: For God doth know that in the day ye eat thereof, then your eyes shall be opened, and ye shall be as gods, knowing good and evil.

Narrator 1

And when the woman saw that the tree was good for food, and that it was pleasant to the eyes, and a tree to be desired to make one wise, she took of the fruit thereof, and did eat, and gave also to her husband with her; and he did eat. And the eyes of them both were opened, and they knew that they were naked; and they sewed fig leaves together, and made themselves aprons. And they heard the voice of the Lord God walking in the garden in the cool of the day: and Adam and his wife hid themselves from the presence of the Lord God.

God  Adam, where art thou?

Adam  I heard thy voice in the garden, and I was afraid, because I was naked; and I hid myself.

God  Who told thee that thou wast naked? Hast thou eaten of the tree, whereof I commanded thee that thou shouldest not eat?

Adam  The woman whom thou gavest to be with me, she gave me of the tree, and I did eat.

God  Woman, what is this that thou hast done?

Eve  The serpent beguiled me and I did eat.

God  *Serpent,* because thou hast done this, thou art cursed above all cattle, and above every beast of the field; upon thy belly shalt thou go, and dust shalt thou eat all the days of thy life: and I will put enmity between thee and the woman, and between thy seed and her seed; it shall bruise thy head, and thou shalt bruise his heel.

Woman, I will greatly multiply thy sorrow and thy conception; in sorrow thou shalt bring forth children; and thy desire shall be to thy husband, and he shall rule over thee.

Adam, because thou hast hearkened unto the voice of thy wife, and hast eaten of the tree, of which I commanded thee, saying, thou shalt not eat of it: cursed is the ground for thy sake; in sorrow shalt thou eat of it all the days of thy life; thorns also and thistles shall it bring forth to thee; and thou shalt eat the herb of the field;

In the sweat of thy face shalt thou eat bread, till thou return unto the ground; for out of it wast thou taken: for dust thou art, and unto dust shalt thou return.

Narrator 2 
And Adam called his wife's name Eve; because she was the mother of all living. Unto Adam also and to his wife did the Lord God make coats of skins, and clothed them.

God (A)
Behold, the man is become as one of us, to know good and evil: and now, lest he put forth his hand, and take also of the tree of life, and eat, and live forever: I shall send him forth from the garden of Eden, to till the ground from whence he was taken.

Narrator 1 (E)
So he drove out the man, and he placed at the east of the garden of Eden Cherubims, and a flaming sword which turned every way, to keep the way of the tree of life.

Ahead of His Time

Joseph

Stage Layout*

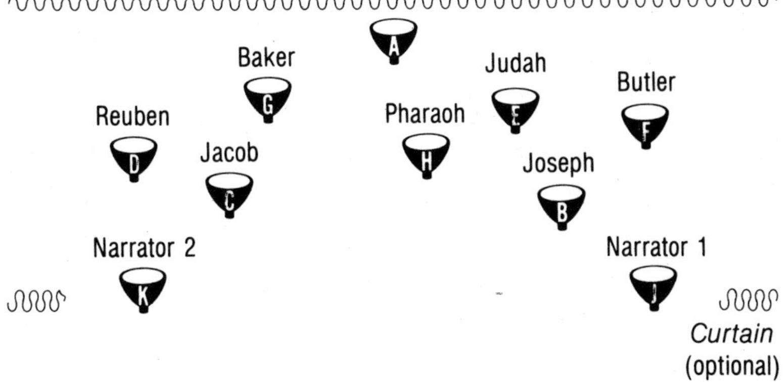

Production Plots

	Lights	Character	Costume	Props
A	White light	God	—	—
B	Blue light	Joseph	Royal blue robe	30-inch stool
C	Straw light	Jacob	Black robe	24-inch ladder
D	Red light	Reuben } (brothers)	Brown robe	24-inch ladder
E	Red light	Judah } (brothers)	Gray robe	24-inch ladder
F	Pink light	Butler & Man (two parts)	Black robe	18-inch stool
G	Pink light	Baker	Black robe	18-inch stool
H	Purple light	Pharaoh	Purple robe	30-inch stool
J	Pink light	Narrator 1	White robe	18-inch stool
K	Pink light	Narrator 2	White robe	18-inch stool

*For Production Notes, see page 9.

Genesis 35:9-41:43

Narrator 1 And God appeared unto Jacob, when he came out of Padan-aram, and blessed him.

God

Thy name is Jacob: thy name shall not be called any more Jacob, but Israel shall be thy name: I am God Almighty: be fruitful and multiply; a nation and a company of nations shall be of thee, and kings shall come out of thy loins; And the land which I gave Abraham and Isaac, to thee I will give it, and to thy seed after thee.

Narrator 2 And Jacob set up a pillar of stone in the place. And Jacob called the name of the place where God spoke to him, Bethel.

Now the sons of Jacob were twelve: Reuben, Simeon, Levi, Judah, Issachar, Zebulun, Joseph, Benjamin, Dan, Naphtali, Gad, and Asher. And Jacob dwelt in the land of Canaan. Joseph, being seventeen years old, was feeding the flock with his brethren.

Narrator 1 Jacob loved Joseph more than all of his children, because he was the son of his old age: and he made him a coat of many colours. When his brethren saw that he loved him more than all his brethren, they hated him, and could not speak peaceably unto him. And Joseph dreamed a dream, and he told it his brethren: and they hated him yet the more.

Joseph Hear, I pray you, this dream which I have dreamed: For, behold, we were binding sheaves in the field, and, lo, my sheaf arose, and also stood upright; and, behold, your sheaves stood round about, and made obeisance to my sheaf.

Brothers Shalt thou indeed reign over us? or shalt thou indeed have dominion over us?

Narrator 2 And they hated him yet the more for his dreams, and for his words.

Joseph Behold, I have dreamed a dream more; and, behold, the sun, and the moon, and the eleven stars made obeisance to me.

Narrator 1 And he told it unto his father, and his father rebuked him.

Jacob What is this dream that thou hast dreamed? Shall I and thy mother and thy brethren indeed come to bow down ourselves to thee?

Narrator 2 And his brethren envied him: but his father observed the saying. His brethren went to feed their father's flock in Shechem.

Jacob Do not thy brethren feed the flock in Shechem? come, and I will send thee unto them.

Joseph Here am I.

Jacob Go, I pray thee, see whether it be well with thy brethren, and well with the flocks; and bring me word again.

Narrator 1 So he sent him to Shechem. And a certain man found him wandering in the field:

Man What seekest thou?

Joseph I seek my brethren: tell me, I pray thee, where they feed their flocks.

Man They are departed hence; for I heard them say, Let us go to Dothan.

Narrator 2 And Joseph went after his brethren, and found them in Dothan. When they saw him afar off, even before he came near unto them, they conspired against him to slay him.

Judah (E) Behold, this dreamer cometh. Come now, therefore, and let us slay him, and cast him into some pit, and we will say, Some evil beast hath devoured him: and we shall see what will become of his dreams.

Narrator 1 (J) And Reuben heard it, and delivered him out of their hands.

Reuben (D) Let us not kill him. Shed no blood, but cast him into this pit that is in the wilderness, and lay no hand upon him.

Narrator 2 (K) . . . that Reuben might rescue him out of their hands, and return him to his father again.

It came to pass, when Joseph was come unto his brethren, that they stript Joseph out of his coat, his coat of many colours that was on him; and they took him, and cast him into a pit: and the pit was empty, and there was no water in it.

And they sat down to eat bread: and they lifted up their eyes and looked, and, behold, a company of Ishmeelites came from Gilead with their camels bearing spicery and balm and myrrh, going to carry it down to Egypt.

Judah (E) What profit is it if we slay our brother, and conceal his blood? Come, and let us sell him to the Ishmeelites, and let not our hand be upon him; for he is our brother, and our flesh.

Narrator 1 (J) And his brethren were content. And they drew and lifted up Joseph out of the pit, and sold Joseph to the Ishmeelites for twenty pieces of silver: and they brought Joseph into Egypt.

And Reuben returned unto the pit; and, behold, Joseph was not in the pit; and he rent his clothes and he returned unto his brethren.

Reuben (D) The child is not; and I, whither shall I go?

Narrator 2 (K) And they took Joseph's coat, and killed a kid of the goats, and dipped the coat in the blood; And they brought it to their father; and said,

Brothers This have we found: know now whether it be thy son's coat or no.

Jacob It is my son's coat; an evil beast hath devoured him; Joseph is without doubt rent in pieces.

Narrator 1 And Jacob rent his clothes, and put sackcloth upon his loins, and mourned for his son many days, and refused to be comforted.

Jacob For I will go down into the grave unto my son mourning.

Narrator 2 Thus his father wept for him. And Joseph was brought down to Egypt; and Potiphar, an officer of Pharaoh, captain of the guard, an Egyptian, bought him of the hands of the Ishmeelites, which had brought him down thither. And the Lord was with Joseph, and he was a prosperous man; and he was in the house of his master the Egyptian. And his master saw that the Lord was with him, and that the Lord made all that he did to prosper in his hand.

Narrator 1 And Joseph found grace in his sight. And it came to pass that from the time that he had made him overseer in his house, and over all that he had, that the Lord blessed the Egyptian's house for Joseph's sake; and the blessing of the Lord was upon all that he had in the house and in the field. Joseph was a goodly person, and well favoured.

And it came to pass after these things, that his master's wife cast her eyes upon Joseph; she said,

Come to me.

Narrator 2 But he refused.

Joseph

Behold, my master knoweth not what is with me in the house, and he hath committed all that he hath to my hand. There is none greater in this house than I; neither hath he kept back anything from me but thee, because thou art his wife: how then can I do this great wickedness, and sin against God?

Narrator 1 J — And she caught him by his garment, and he left his garment in her hand, and fled, and got him out. And Joseph's master, Potiphar, took him, and put him into the prison, a place where the king's prisoners were bound. But the Lord was with Joseph, and shewed him mercy, and gave him favour in the sight of the keeper of the prison. And the keeper of the prison committed to Joseph's hand all the prisoners that were in the prison.

The keeper of the prison looked not to anything that was under his hand; because the Lord was with him, and that which he did, the Lord made it to prosper.

Narrator 2 K — And it came to pass that the butler of the king of Egypt and his baker had offended their Lord, the king of Egypt. And Pharaoh was wroth against two of his officers. He put them into the prison, the place where Joseph was bound. And the captain of the guard charged Joseph with them, and he served them: and they continued a season in prison.

Narrator 1 J — They dreamed a dream, each man his dream in one night, the butler and the baker of the king of Egypt, which were bound in the prison. And Joseph came in unto them in the morning, and looked upon them, and, behold, they were sad.

Joseph B — Wherefore look ye so sadly today?

Butler & Baker F G — We have dreamed a dream, and there is no interpreter of it.

Joseph B — Do not interpretations belong to God? Tell me them, I pray you.

Butler F — In my dream, behold, a vine was before me. In the vine there were three branches: and it was as though it budded, and her blossoms shot forth; and the clusters thereof brought forth ripe grapes: Pharaoh's cup was in my hand: and I took the grapes, and pressed them into Pharaoh's cup, and I gave the cup into Pharaoh's hand.

Joseph This is the interpretation of it: The three branches are three days: yet within three days shall Pharaoh lift up thine head, and restore thee unto thy place: and thou shalt deliver Pharaoh's cup into his hand, after the former manner when thou wast his butler.

But think on me when it shall be well with thee, and show kindness, I pray thee, unto me, and make mention of me unto Pharaoh, and bring me out of this house: for indeed I was stolen away out of the land of the Hebrews: and here also have I done nothing that they should put me into the dungeon.

Narrator 2 When the chief baker saw that the interpretation was good, he said unto Joseph,

Baker I also was in my dream, and, behold, I had three white baskets on my head: And in the uppermost basket there was all manner of bakemeats for Pharaoh; and the birds did eat them out of the basket upon my head.

Joseph This is the interpretation thereof: The three baskets are three days: yet within three days shall Pharaoh lift up thy head from off thee, and shall hang thee on a tree; and the birds shall eat thy flesh from off thee.

Narrator 1 And it came to pass the third day, which was Pharaoh's birthday, that he made a feast unto all his servants. And he restored the chief butler unto his butlership again; and he gave the cup into Pharaoh's hand: But he hanged the chief baker: as Joseph had interpreted to them. Yet did not the chief butler remember Joseph, but forgot him.

It came to pass at the end of two full years that Pharaoh dreamed. In the morning his spirit was troubled.

Butler There was with us (in the prison) a young man, an Hebrew, servant to the captain of the guard; and he interpreted to us our dreams.

Narrator 2 Then Pharaoh sent and called Joseph, and they brought him hastily out of the dungeon: and he shaved himself, and changed his raiment, and came in unto Pharaoh.

Pharaoh Joseph, I have dreamed a dream, and there is none that can interpret it. I have heard say of thee, that thou canst understand a dream to interpret it.

Joseph It is not in me: God shall give Pharaoh an answer of peace.

Pharaoh In my dream, behold, I stood upon the bank of the river: behold, there came out of the river seven kine, fatfleshed and well favoured; and they fed in a meadow:

And, behold, seven other kine came up after them, poor, and very ill favoured and leanfleshed, such as I never saw in all the land of Egypt for badness: And the lean and the ill favoured kine did eat up the first seven fat kine. And when they had eaten them up, it could not be known that they had eaten them; but they were still ill favoured, as at the beginning. So I awoke. And I saw in my dream, and, behold, seven ears came up in one stalk, full and good: And behold, seven ears, withered, thin, and blasted with the east wind, sprung up after them:

The thin ears devoured the seven good ears: I told this unto the magicians; but there was none that could declare it to me.

Joseph God hath shewed Pharaoh what he is about to do. The seven good kine are seven years; and the seven good ears are seven years: the dream is one.

The seven thin and ill favoured kine that came up after them are seven years; and the seven empty ears, blasted with the east wind, shall be seven years of famine. This is the thing which I have spoken unto Pharaoh: what God is about to do he sheweth unto Pharaoh.

Behold, there come seven years of great plenty throughout all the land of Egypt. There shall arise after them seven years of famine; and all the plenty shall be forgotten in the land of Egypt; and the famine shall consume the land; the plenty shall not be known in the land by reason of that famine following; for it shall be very grievous. And for that the dream was doubled unto Pharaoh twice; it is because the thing is established by God, and God will shortly bring it to pass.

Now, therefore, let Pharaoh pick out a man discreet and wise, and set him over the land of Egypt. Let Pharaoh do this, and let him appoint officers over the land, and take up the fifth part of the land of Egypt in the seven plenteous years. And let them gather all the food of those good years that come, and lay up corn under the hand of Pharaoh, and let them keep food in the cities. And that food shall be for store to the land against the seven years of famine, which shall be in the land of Egypt; that the land perish not through the famine.

Narrator 1 (J) And the thing was good in the eyes of Pharaoh, and in the eyes of the servants.

Pharaoh (H) Can we find such a one as this is, a man in whom the spirit of God is?

Joseph, forasmuch as God hath shewed thee all this, there is none so discreet and wise as thou art: Thou shalt be over my house, and according unto thy word shall all my people be ruled: only in the throne will I be greater than thou. See, I have set thee over all the land of Egypt.

Narrator 2 (K) And Pharaoh took off his ring from his hand, and put it upon Joseph's hand, and arrayed him in vestures of fine linen, and put a gold chain about his neck; and he made him to ride in the second chariot which he had; and he made him ruler over all the land of Egypt.

Pharaoh (H) I am Pharaoh, and without thee, Joseph, shall no man lift up his hand or foot in all the land of Egypt.

Returning Good for Evil

Joseph

Stage Layout*

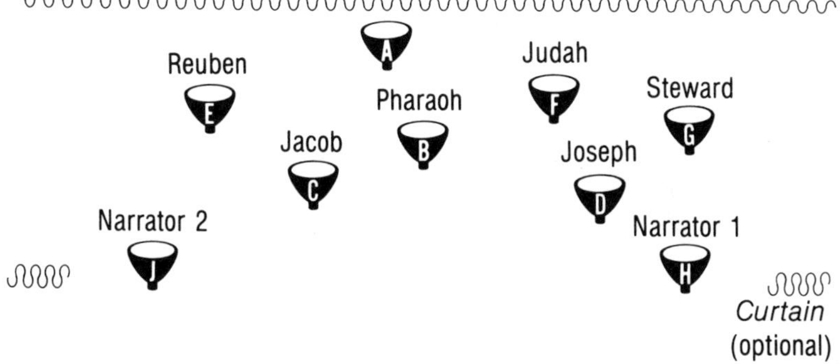

Production Plots

	Lights	Character	Costume	Props
A	White light	God	—	—
B	Purple light	Pharaoh	Purple robe	30-inch stool
C	Straw light	Jacob	Black robe	24-inch ladder
D	Blue light	Joseph	Royal blue robe	30-inch stool
E	Red light	Reuben } (brothers)	Brown robe	24-inch ladder
F	Red light	Judah } (brothers)	Gray robe	24-inch ladder
G	Yellow light	Steward	Black robe	18-inch stool
H	Pink light	Narrator 1	White robe	18-inch stool
J	Pink light	Narrator 2	White robe	18-inch stool

*For Production Notes, see page 9.

Genesis 41-50

Pharaoh (B) I am Pharaoh, and without thee, Joseph, shall no man lift up his hand or foot in all the land of Egypt.

Narrator 1 (H) Joseph was thirty years old when he stood before Pharaoh king of Egypt. And Joseph went out from the presence of Pharaoh, and went throughout all the land of Egypt. And in the seven plenteous years the earth brought forth by handfuls. And he gathered up all the food of the seven years, which were in the land of Egypt, and laid up the food in the cities: the food of the field, which was round about every city, laid he up. And Joseph gathered corn as the sand of the sea, very much, until he stopped numbering; for it was without number.

The seven years of plenteousness, that was in the land of Egypt, were ended. And the seven years of dearth began to come, as Joseph had said: and the dearth was in all lands; but in the land of Egypt there was bread.

When all the land of Egypt was famished, the people cried to Pharaoh for bread.

Pharaoh (B) Go unto Joseph; what he saith to you, do.

Narrator 2 (J) And the famine was over all the face of the earth: And Joseph opened all the storehouses, and sold unto the Egyptians; and the famine waxed sore in the land. And all countries came into Egypt to Joseph for to buy corn; because that the famine was so sore in all lands. Now when Jacob saw that there was corn in Egypt, Jacob said unto his sons . . .

Jacob (C) Why do ye look upon another? Behold, I have heard that there is corn in Egypt: get you down thither, and buy for us; that we may live, and not die.

Narrator 1 (H) And Joseph's ten brethren went down to buy corn in Egypt. But Benjamin, Joseph's brother, Jacob sent not with his brethren.

Jacob (C) Lest peradventure mischief befall him.

Narrator 2 (J) And the sons of Israel came to buy corn: for the famine was in all the land of Canaan. Joseph was the governor over the land, and he it was that sold to all the people of the land: Joseph's brethren came, and bowed down themselves before him. Joseph saw his brethren, and he knew them, but made himself strange unto them, and spake roughly unto them;

Joseph (D) Whence come ye?

Reuben (E) From the land of Canaan to buy food.

Narrator 1 (H) Joseph knew his brethren, but they knew not him. And Joseph remembered the dreams which he dreamed of them.

Joseph (D) Ye are spies; to see the nakedness of the land ye are come.

Judah (F) Nay, my Lord, but to buy food are thy servants come. We are all one man's sons; we are true men, thy servants are no spies.

Joseph (D) Nay, but to see the nakedness of the land ye are come.

Reuben (E) Thy servants are twelve brethren, the sons of one man in the land of Canaan; and behold, the youngest is this day with our father, and one is not.

Joseph (D) That is it that I spake unto you, saying, Ye are spies: Hereby ye shall be proved: By the life of Pharaoh ye shall not go forth hence, except your youngest brother come hither. Send one of you, and let him fetch your brother, and ye shall be kept in prison, that your words may be proved, whether there be any truth in you: or else, by the life of Pharaoh, surely ye are spies.

Narrator 2 J — And he put them all together into ward three days. And on the third day, Joseph said. . .

Joseph D — This do, and live; for I fear God: If ye be true men, let one of your brethren be bound in the house of your prison: go ye, carry corn for the famine of your houses: But bring your youngest brother unto me; so shall your words be verified, and ye shall not die.

Judah F — We are verily guilty concerning our brother, in that we saw the anguish of his soul, when he besought us, and we would not hear; therefore is this distress come upon us.

Reuben E — Spake I not unto you, saying, Do not sin against the child; and ye would not hear? therefore, behold, also his blood is required.

Narrator 1 H — And they knew not that Joseph understood them; for he spake unto them by an interpreter. And Joseph turned himself about from them, and wept; and returned to them again, and communed with them, and took from them Simeon, and bound him before their eyes.

Then Joseph commanded to fill their sacks with corn, and to restore every man's money into his sack, and to give them provision for the way. And they laded their asses with the corn, and departed thence.

And as one of them opened his sack to give his ass provender in the inn, he spied his money; for, behold, it was in his sack's mouth.

Judah F — My money is restored; and, lo, it is even in my sack.

Reuben E — What is this that God hath done unto us?

Narrator 2 J — And they came unto Jacob their father unto the land of Canaan, and told him all that befell unto them;

Judah F — The man, who is the lord of the land, spake roughly to us, and took us for spies of the country. We said unto him, We are true men; we are no spies. We be twelve brethren, sons of our father; one is not, and the youngest is this day with our father in the land of Canaan.

Reuben The man, the lord of the country, said unto us, Hereby shall I know that ye are true men; leave one of your brethren here with me, and take food for the famine of your households, and be gone.

And bring your youngest brother unto me: then shall I know that ye are no spies, but that ye are true men: so will I deliver you your brother, and ye shall do business in the land.

Narrator 1 And it came to pass as they emptied their sacks, that, behold, every man's bundle of money was in his sack: and when both they and their father saw the bundles of money, they were afraid.

Jacob Me have ye bereaved of my children: Joseph is not, and Simeon is not, and ye will take Benjamin away: all these things are against me.

Reuben Slay my two sons, if I bring him not to thee: deliver him into my hand, and I will bring him to thee again.

Jacob My son shall not go down with you; for his brother is dead, and he is left alone: if mischief befall him by the way in the which ye go, then shall ye bring down my gray hairs with sorrow to the grave.

Narrator 2 And the famine was sore in the land. And it came to pass, when they had eaten up the corn which they had brought out of Egypt, their father said . . .

Jacob 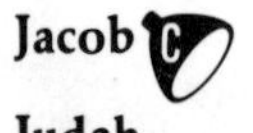

Go again, buy us a little food.

Judah

The man did solemnly protest unto us, saying, Ye shall not see my face, except your brother be with you. If thou wilt send our brother with us, we will go down and buy thee food: But if thou wilt not send him, we will not go down.

Jacob

Wherefore dealt ye so ill with me, as to tell the man whether ye had yet a brother?

Judah

The man asked us of our state, and of our kindred, saying, Is your father yet alive? have ye another brother? and we told him according to the tenor of these words: could we certainly know that he would say, Bring your brother down?

Send the lad with me, and we will arise and go; that we may live, and not die. I will be surety for him; of my hand shalt thou require him: if I bring him not unto thee, then let me bear the blame forever.

Jacob C

If it must be so now, do this; take of the best fruits in the land in your vessels, and carry down the man a present, a little balm, and a little honey, spices, and myrrh, nuts, and almonds: take double money in your hand; and the money that was brought again in the mouth of your sacks, carry it again in your hand; peradventure it was an oversight: Take also your brother, and arise, go again unto the man: God Almighty give you mercy before the man, that he may send away your other brother, and Benjamin. If I be bereaved of my children, I am bereaved.

Narrator 1 H

And the men took that present, and they took double money in their hand, and Benjamin; and rose up, and went down to Egypt, and stood before Joseph. When Joseph saw Benjamin with them, he said to the ruler of the house . . .

Joseph D

Bring these men home, and slay, and make ready; for these men shall dine with me at noon.

Narrator 2 J

And the man did as Joseph bade; and the man brought the brethren into Joseph's house.

Reuben E

Because of the money that was returned in our sacks at the first time are we brought in; that he may seek occasion against us, and fall upon us, and take us for bondmen.

Narrator 1 H

And they came near to the steward of Joseph's house, and they communed with him at the door of the house.

Judah F

O sir, we came indeed down at the first time to buy food: and it came to pass, when we came to the inn, that we opened our sacks, and, behold, every man's money was in the mouth of his sack, our money in full weight: and we have brought it again in our hand. Other money have we brought down in our hands to buy food: we cannot tell who put our money in our sacks.

Steward G — Peace be to you, fear not: your God, and the God of your father, hath given you treasure in your sacks: I had your money.

Narrator 2 J — And he brought Simeon out unto them. And the man brought the brethren into Joseph's house, and gave them water, and they washed their feet; and he gave their asses provender.

And they made ready the present to give to Joseph when he should come at noon: for they heard that they should eat bread there. And when Joseph came home, they brought him the present, and bowed themselves to him.

Joseph D — Is your father well, the old man of whom ye spake? Is he yet alive?

Reuben E — Thy servant our father is in good health, he is yet alive.

Narrator 1 H — And he lifted up his eyes, and saw his brother Benjamin.

Joseph D — Is this your younger brother, of whom ye spake unto me? God be gracious unto thee, my son.

Narrator 2 J — And Joseph made haste; for his bowels did yearn upon his brother: and he sought where to weep; and he entered into his chamber, and wept there. And he washed his face, and went out, and said . . .

Joseph D — Set on bread.

Narrator 1 H — And they sat before him, the firstborn according to his birthright, and the youngest according to his youth: and the men marvelled one at another. And they drank, and were merry with him. And he commanded the steward of his house . . .

Joseph D — Fill the men's sacks with food, as much as they can carry, and put every man's money in his sack's mouth. Put my cup, the silver cup, in the sack's mouth of the youngest, and his corn money.

Narrator 2 J As soon as the morning was light, the men were sent away, they and their asses.

Joseph D Up, follow after the men; and when thou dost overtake them, say unto them, Wherefore have ye rewarded evil for good? Is not this the cup in which my lord drinketh, and whereby indeed he uses it to foretell the future? ye have done evil in so doing.

Narrator 1 H The steward overtook them, and he spake unto them these same words.

Judah F Wherefore saith my lord these words? God forbid that thy servants should do according to this thing. Behold, the money, which we found in our sacks' mouths, we brought again unto thee out of the land of Canaan: how then should we steal out of thy lord's house silver or gold? With whomsoever of thy servants it be found, both let him die, and we also will be my lord's bondmen.

Steward G Also let it be according unto your words: he with whom it is found shall be my servant; and ye shall be blameless.

Narrator 2 J Then they speedily took down every man his sack to the ground, and opened every man his sack. He searched, and began at the eldest, and left at the youngest: and the cup was found in Benjamin's sack.

They rent their clothes, and laded every man his ass, and returned to the city. Judah and his brethren came to Joseph's house; for he was yet there: and they fell before him on the ground.

Joseph D What deed is this, that ye have done? know ye not that such a man as I can certainly divine?

Judah F What shall we say unto my lord? what shall we speak? or how shall we clear ourselves? God hath found out the iniquity of thy servants, both we, and he also with whom the cup is found.

Joseph D God forbid that I should do so: but the man in whose hand the cup is found, he shall be my servant; and as for you, get you up in peace unto your father.

Judah

Oh, my lord, let thy servant, I pray thee, speak a word in my lord's ears, and let not thine anger burn against thy servant: for thou art even as Pharaoh.

My lord asked his servants, saying, Have ye a father, or a brother? And we said unto my lord, We have a father, an old man, and a child of his old age, a little one; and his brother is dead, and he alone is left of his mother, and his father loveth him. And thou saidst unto thy servants, Bring him down unto me, that I may set mine eyes upon him. And we said unto my lord, The lad cannot leave his father: for if he should leave his father, his father would die. And thou saidst unto thy servants, Except your youngest brother come down with you, ye shall see my face no more.

And it came to pass, when we came up unto thy servant my father, we told him the words of my lord. And our father said, Go again and buy us a little food. And we said, We cannot go down: if our youngest brother be with us, then will we go down: for we may not see the man's face, except our youngest brother be with us.

And thy servant my father said unto us, Ye know that my wife bare me two sons: And the one went out from me, and I said, Surely he is torn to pieces; and I saw him not since: And if ye take this also from me, and mischief befall him, ye shall bring down my gray hairs with sorrow to the grave. For thy servant became surety for the lad unto my father, saying, If I bring him not unto thee, then I shall bear the blame to my father forever.

I pray thee, let thy servant abide instead of the lad, a bondman to my lord; and let the lad go up with his brethren. How shall I go up to my father, and the lad be not with me? lest peradventure I see the evil that shall come on my father.

Narrator 1 Then Joseph could not refrain himself before all them that stood by him; and he cried . . .

Joseph Cause every man to go out from me.

Narrator 2 He wept aloud: and the Egyptians and Pharaoh heard.

Joseph I am Joseph. Doth my father yet live?

Narrator 1 His brethren could not answer him; for they were troubled by his presence.

Joseph Come near to me, I pray you. I am Joseph, your brother, whom ye sold into Egypt. Now be not grieved, nor angry with yourselves, that ye sold me hither; for God did send me before you to preserve life.

For these two years hath the famine been in the land: and yet there are five years, in the which there shall neither be earing nor harvest. God sent me before you to preserve you a posterity in the earth, and to save your lives by a great deliverance. It was not you that sent me hither, but God: and he hath made me a father to Pharaoh, and lord of all his house, and a ruler throughout all the land of Egypt.

Haste ye, and go up to my father, and say unto him, Thus saith thy son Joseph, God hath made me lord of all Egypt: come down unto me, tarry not: thou shalt dwell in the land of Goshen, and thou shalt be near unto me, thou, and thy children, and thy children's children, and thy flocks, and thy herds, and all that thou hast.

There will I nourish thee; for yet there are five years of famine; lest thou, and all that thou hast, come to poverty. Behold, your eyes see, and the eyes of my brother Benjamin, that it is my mouth that speaketh unto you. Ye shall tell my father of all my glory in Egypt, and of all that ye have seen; and ye shall haste and bring down my father hither.

Narrator 2 And he fell upon his brother Benjamin's neck, and wept. He kissed all his brethren, and wept upon them: after that his brethren talked with him. The fame thereof was heard in Pharaoh's house, saying, Joseph's brethren are come: and it pleased Pharaoh well, and his servants.

Pharaoh Joseph, Say unto thy brethren, This do ye; load your beasts, and go, get you unto the land of Canaan. Take your father, and your households, and come unto me: I will give you the good of the land of Egypt, and ye shall eat the fat of the land. Thou art commanded, this do ye; take you wagons out of the land of Egypt for your little ones, and for your wives, and bring your father, and come. Also regard not your stuff; for the good of all the land of Egypt is yours.

Narrator 1 And the children of Jacob did so: and Joseph gave them wagons, according to the commandment of Pharaoh, and gave them provision for the way. So he sent his brethren away. They went up out of Egypt, and came into the land of Canaan unto Jacob their father.

Reuben Joseph is yet alive, and he is governor over all the land of Egypt.

Narrator 2 Jacob's heart fainted for he believed them not. And they told him all the words of Joseph, and when he saw the wagons which Joseph had sent to carry him, the spirit of Jacob their father revived.

Jacob It is enough; Joseph my son is yet alive: I will go and see him before I die.

Narrator 1 And God spake unto Jacob in the visions of the night.

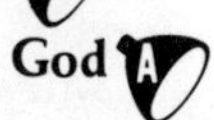

God Jacob, Jacob . . .

Jacob Here am I.

God I am God, the God of thy father: fear not to go down into Egypt, for I will there make of thee a great nation: I will go down with thee into Egypt; and Joseph shall put his hand upon thine eyes.

Narrator 2 And Jacob rose up from Beersheba: and the sons carried Jacob, their father, their little ones, and their wives, in the wagons which Pharaoh had sent to carry him. And they took their cattle, and their goods, which they had gotten in the land of Canaan, and came into Egypt, Jacob and all his seed with him.

Jacob C — Forgive, I pray thee now, the trespass of thy brethren, and their sin; for they did unto thee evil: and now, we pray thee, forgive the trespass of the servants of the God of thy father.

Narrator 1 H — And Joseph wept when they spake unto him. And his brethren also went and fell down before his face.

Brothers E F — Behold, we be thy servants.

Joseph D — Fear not; for am I in the place of God? But as for you, ye thought evil against me; but God meant it unto good. Now, therefore, fear ye not: I will nourish you, and your little ones.

Narrator 2 J — He comforted them, and spake kindly unto them. And Joseph lived an hundred and ten years.

Loyalty Pays

The Book of Ruth

Stage Layout*

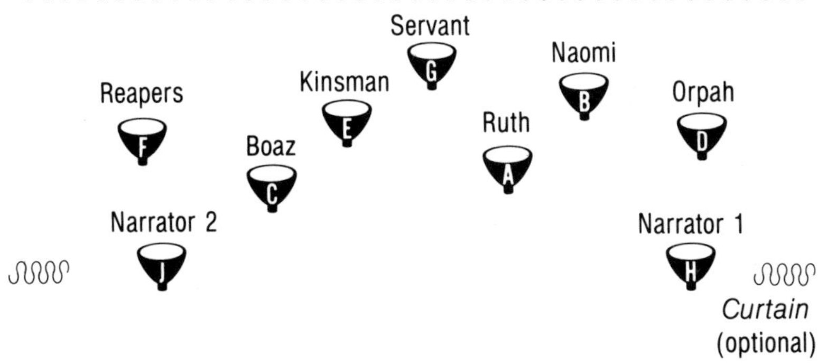

Production Plots

	Lights	Character	Costume	Props
A	Blue light	Ruth	Light blue robe	30-inch stool
B	White light	Naomi	Pink robe	24-inch ladder
C	Blue light	Boaz	Dark blue robe	30-inch stool
D	Red light	Orpah & Women (two parts)	Gray robe	18-inch stool
E	Yellow light	Kinsman	Brown robe	24-inch ladder
F	Red light	Reapers (People)	Brown robe	18-inch stool
G	Straw light	Servant	Black robe	18-inch stool
H	White light	Narrator 1	White robe	18-inch stool
J	White light	Narrator 2	White robe	18-inch stool

*For Production Notes, see page 9.

The Book of Ruth

Narrator 1 H

Now it came to pass in the days when the judges ruled, that there was a famine in the land. And a certain man of Bethlehem-judah went to sojourn in the country of Moab, he, and his wife, and his two sons. And the name of the man was Elimelech, and the name of his wife Naomi, and the name of his two sons Mahlon and Chilion. And they came into the country of Moab, and continued there.

Narrator 2 J

And Elimelech, Naomi's husband, died; and she was left, and her two sons. And they took them wives of the women of Moab; the name of the one was Orpah, and the name of the other Ruth: and they dwelled there about ten years.

And Mahlon and Chilion died also, both of them; and the woman was left of her two sons and her husband.

Narrator 1 H

Then she arose, with her daughters-in-law, that she might return from the country of Moab: for she had heard in the country of Moab how that the Lord had visited his people in giving them bread.

Wherefore she went forth out of the place where she was, and her two daughters-in-law with her; and they went on the way to return to the land of Judah.

Naomi B

Go, return each to her mother's house: the Lord deal kindly with you as ye have dealt with the dead, and with me. The Lord grant you that ye may find rest, each of you in the house of her husband.

Narrator 2 J Then she kissed them; and they lifted up their voice and wept.

Orpah/Ruth A D Surely we will return with thee unto thy people.

Naomi B Turn again, my daughters: why will ye go with me? are there yet any more sons in my womb, that they may be your husbands? Turn again, my daughters, go your way; for I am too old to have an husband. If I should say, I have hope, if I should have an husband also tonight, and should bear also sons; would ye tarry for them till they were grown? nay, my daughters; for it grieveth me much, for your sakes, that the hand of the Lord is gone out against me.

Narrator 1 H They lifted up their voices and wept again: Orpah kissed her mother-in-law; but Ruth clave unto her.

Naomi B Behold, thy sister-in-law is gone back unto her people, and unto her gods: return thou after thy sister-in-law.

Ruth A Entreat me not to leave thee, or to return from following after thee: for whither thou goest, I will go; and where thou lodgest, I will lodge: thy people shall be my people, and thy God my God: Where thou diest, will I die, and there will I be buried: the Lord do so to me, and more also, if ought but death part thee and me.

Narrator 2 J When she saw that she was stedfastly minded to go with her, then she left speaking unto her. So they two went until they came to Bethlehem. And it came to pass, when they were come to Bethlehem, that all the city was moved about them.

Women D Is this Naomi?

Naomi B Call me not Naomi, call me Mara: for the Almighty hath dealt very bitterly with me. I went out full, and the Lord hath brought me home again empty: why then call ye me Naomi, seeing the Lord hath testified against me, and the Almighty hath afflicted me.

Narrator 1 H And they came to Bethlehem in the beginning of barley harvest. Naomi had a kinsman of her husband's, a mighty man of wealth, of the family of Elimelech; and his name was Boaz.

Ruth Let me now go to the field, and glean ears of corn after him in whose sight I shall find grace.

Naomi Go, my daughter.

Narrator 2 And she went, and came, and gleaned in the field after the reapers: and she came to a part of the field belonging unto Boaz, who was of the kindred of Elimelech. And, behold, Boaz came from Bethlehem and said unto the reapers . . .

Boaz The Lord be with you.

Reapers The Lord bless thee.

Boaz Whose damsel is this?

Servant It is the Moabitish damsel that came back with Naomi out of the country of Moab.

Ruth I pray you, let me glean and gather after the reapers among the sheaves.

Boaz Hearest thou not, my daughter? Go not to glean in another field, neither go from hence, but abide here fast by my maidens. Let thine eyes be on the field that they do reap, and go thou after them: have I not charged the young men that they shall not touch thee? and when thou art athirst, go unto the vessels, and drink of that which the young men have drawn.

Ruth

Why have I found grace in thine eyes, that thou shouldest take knowledge of me, seeing I am a stranger?

Boaz

It hath fully been shewed me, all that thou hast done unto thy mother-in-law since the death of thine husband: and how thou hast left thy father and mother, and the land of thy nativity, and art come unto a people which thou knewest not heretofore. The Lord recompense thy work, and a full reward be given thee of the Lord God of Israel, under whose wings thou art come to trust.

Ruth

Let me find favor in thy sight, my lord; for that thou hast comforted me, and for that thou hast spoken friendly unto thine handmaid, though I be not like unto one of thine handmaidens.

Boaz At mealtime come thou hither, and eat of the bread, and dip thy morsel in the vinegar.

Narrator 1 And when she was risen up to glean . . .

Boaz Let her glean even among the sheaves, and reproach her not: and let fall also some of the handfuls of purpose for her, and leave them, that she may glean them, and rebuke her not.

Narrator 2 So she gleaned in the field until evening. Then she beat out what she had gleaned: and it was about an ephah of barley. And she took it up and went into the city, and gave it to Naomi.

Naomi Where hast thou gleaned today and where wroughtest thou? blessed be he that did take knowledge of thee.

Ruth The man's name with whom I wrought today is Boaz.

Naomi Blessed be he of the Lord, who hath not left off his kindness to the living and to the dead. The man is near of kin unto us, one of our next kinsmen.

Ruth He said unto me also, Thou shalt keep fast by my young men, until they have ended all my harvest.

Naomi It is good, my daughter, that you go out with his maidens, that they meet thee not in any other field.

Narrator 1 So she kept fast by the maidens of Boaz to glean unto the end of barley harvest, and of wheat harvest; and dwelt with her mother-in-law.

* * *

Naomi My daughter, shall I not seek rest for thee, that it may be well with thee? Is not Boaz of our kindred, with whose maidens thou wast? Behold, he winnoweth barley tonight in the threshing-floor. Wash thyself, therefore, and anoint thee, and put thy raiment upon thee, and get thee down to the floor: but make not thyself known unto the man, until he shall have done eating and drinking. And it shall be, when he lieth down, that thou shalt mark the place where he shall lie, and thou shalt go in, and uncover his feet, and lay thee down; and he will tell thee what thou shalt do.

Ruth A All that thou sayest unto me I will do.

Narrator 2 J So she went down unto the floor, and did according to all that her mother-in-law bade her. And when Boaz had eaten and drunk, and his heart was merry, he went to lie down at the end of the heap of corn: and she came softly, and uncovered his feet, and laid her down. And it came to pass at midnight, that the man was afraid, and turned himself: and, behold, a woman lay at his feet.

Boaz C Who art thou?

Ruth A I am Ruth thine handmaid; spread therefore thy skirt over thine handmaid; for thou art a near kinsman.

Boaz C Blessed be thou of the Lord, my daughter: for thou hast shewed more kindness in the latter end than at the beginning, inasmuch as thou followedst not young men, whether poor or rich. Fear not; I will do to thee all that thou requirest: for all the city of my people doth know that thou art a virtuous woman. It is true that I am thy near kinsman: howbeit, there is a kinsman nearer than I.

Tarry this night, and it shall be in the morning, that if he will perform unto thee the part of a kinsman, well; let him do the kinsman's part: but if he will not do the part of a kinsman to thee, then will I do the part of a kinsman to thee, as the Lord liveth: lie down until the morning.

Narrator 1 H And she lay at his feet until the morning: and she rose up before one could know another.

Boaz C Let it not be known that a woman came into the floor. Bring the veil that thou hast upon thee, and hold it.

Narrator 2 J When she held it, he measured six measures of barley and laid it on her: and she went into the city to her mother-in-law.

Naomi How did it go, my daughter?

Ruth These six measures of barley gave he me: for he said to me, Go not empty unto thy mother-in-law.

Naomi Sit still, my daughter, until thou know how the matter will fall: for the man will not be in rest, until he have finished the thing this day.

Narrator 1 Then went Boaz up to the gate, and sat him down there: and, behold, the kinsman, of whom Boaz spake, came by.

Boaz Ho, such a one! turn aside, sit down here.

Narrator 1 And he took ten men of the elders of the city, And they sat down. And he said unto the kinsman . . .

Boaz Naomi, that is come again out of the country of Moab, selleth a parcel of land, which was our brother Elimelech's: And I thought to advertise thee, saying, Buy it before the inhabitants, and before the elders of my people. If thou wilt redeem it, redeem it: but if thou wilt not redeem it, then tell me, that I may know: for there is none to redeem it beside thee: and I am after thee.

Kinsman I will redeem it.

Boaz What day thou buyest the field of the hand of Naomi, thou must buy it also of Ruth the Moabitess, the wife of the dead, to raise up the name of the dead upon his inheritance.

Kinsman I cannot redeem it for myself, lest I mar mine own inheritance: redeem thou my right to thyself: for I cannot redeem it.

Narrator 2 Now this was the manner in former times in Israel concerning redeeming and changing, to confirm all things: a man plucked off his shoe, and gave it to his neighbour: and this was a testimony in Israel. So he drew off his shoe. And Boaz said unto the elders, and unto all the people,

Boaz

Ye are witnesses this day, that I have bought all that was Elimelech's, and all that was Chilion's and Mahlon's, of the hand of Naomi. Moreover, Ruth the Moabitess, the wife of Mahlon, have I purchased to be my wife, to raise up the name of the dead upon his inheritance, that the name of the dead be not cut off from among his brethren, and from the gate of his place: ye are witnesses this day.

Narrator 1

All the people that were in the gate, and the elders, said . . .

People

We are witnesses. The Lord make the woman that is come into thine house like Rachel and like Leah, which two did build the house of Israel: and do thou worthily in Ephratah, and be famous in Bethlehem. And let thy house be like the house of Pharez, of the seed which the Lord shall give thee of this young woman.

Narrator 2

So Boaz took Ruth and she was his wife: And the women said unto Naomi . . .

Women

Blessed be the Lord, which hath not left thee this day without a kinsman, that his name may be famous in Israel.

Elijah—God—Fire

Elijah and The Prophets of Baal

Stage Layout*

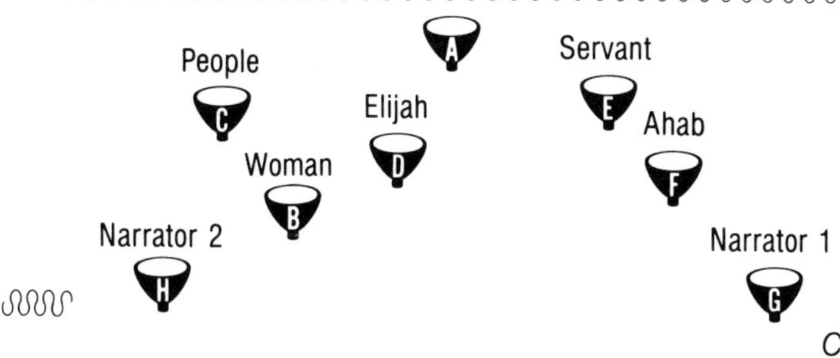

Production Plots

	Lights	Character	Costume	Props
A	White light	God	—	—
B	Blue light	Woman	Light blue robe	30-inch stool
C	Purple light	People	Dark blue robe	can use a 20-inch bench for 3 people
D	White light	Elijah	Black robe	24-inch ladder
E	Straw light	Servant	Yellow robe	18-inch stool
F	Red light	Ahab	Red robe	30-inch stool
G	Pink light	Narrator 1	White robe	18-inch stool
H	Pink light	Narrator 2	White robe	18-inch stool

*For Production Notes, see page 9.

I Kings 16:29-18:45

Narrator 1 G
And in the thirty and eighth year of Asa, king of Judah, began Ahab the son of Omri to reign over Israel. And Ahab reigned over Israel in Samaria twenty and two years.

Narrator 2 H
Ahab did more to provoke the Lord God of Israel to anger than all the kings of Israel that were before him. And Elijah the Tishbite said unto Ahab . . .

Elijah D
As the Lord God of Israel liveth, there shall not be dew nor rain these years, but according to my word.

God A
Get thee hence—turn thee eastward, and hide thyself by the brook Cherith that is before Jordan. And it shall be that thou shalt drink of the brook; and I have commanded the ravens to feed thee there.

Narrator 1 G
So he went and did according unto the word of the Lord: for he went and dwelt by the brook Cherith, and the ravens brought him bread and flesh in the morning, and bread and flesh in the evening; and he drank of the brook.

Narrator 2 H
And it came to pass after awhile that the brook dried up, because there had been no rain in the land. And the word of the Lord came unto him, saying

God A
Arise, get thee to Zeraphath, and dwell there. Behold, I have commanded a widow there to sustain thee.

Narrator 1 G
So he arose and went to Zeraphath. And when he came to the gate of the city, the widow woman was there gathering sticks.

Elijah D — Fetch me, I pray thee, a little water in a vessel, that I may drink. Bring me a morsel of bread in thine hand.

Woman B — As the Lord thy God liveth, I have not a cake but an handful of meal in a barrel, and a little oil in a cruse: and, behold, I am gathering two sticks, that I may go in and dress it for me and my son, that we may eat it, and die.

Elijah D — Fear not; go and do as thou hast said: but make me thereof a little cake first, and bring it unto me, and after make for thee and for thy son. For thus saith the Lord God of Israel, The barrel of meal shall not waste, neither shall the cruse of oil fail, until the day that the Lord sendeth rain upon the earth.

Narrator 2 H — And she went and did according to the saying of Elijah: and she, and he, and her house, did eat many days. And the barrel of meal wasted not, neither did the cruse of oil fail, according to the word of the Lord.

Narrator 1 G — After many days the word of the Lord came to Elijah.

God A — Go, shew thyself unto Ahab; and I will send rain upon the earth.

Ahab F — Art thou he that troubleth Israel?

Elijah D — I have not troubled Israel; but thou, and thy father's house. Ye have forsaken the commandments of the Lord, and thou hast followed Baalim. Now gather to me all Israel unto mount Carmel, and the prophets of Baal, four hundred and fifty, and the prophets of the groves four hundred, which eat at Jezebel's table.

Narrator 2 H — So Ahab sent unto all the children of Israel, and gathered the prophets together unto mount Carmel.

Narrator 1 G — And Elijah came unto all the people, and said

Elijah D — How long halt ye between two opinions? if the Lord be God, follow him: but if Baal, then follow him.

Narrator 2 H — The people answered him not a word.

Elijah D — I, even I only, remain a prophet of the Lord; but Baal's prophets are four hundred and fifty men. Let them therefore give us two bullocks; and let them choose one bullock for themselves, and cut it in pieces, and lay it on wood, and put no fire under. Call ye on the name of your gods, and I will call on the name of the Lord. The God that answereth by fire, let him be God.

People (C) It is well spoken.
Let it be so.
I am willing.

Narrator 2 (H) And Elijah said unto the prophets of Baal,

Elijah (D) Choose you one bullock for yourselves, and dress it first, for ye are many; and call on the name of your gods, but put no fire under.

Narrator 1 (G) They took the bullock which was given them, and they dressed it, and called on the name of Baal from morning even until noon.

Prophets (People) (C) O Baal, hear us! O Baal, hear us!
O Baal, hear us!

Narrator 2 (H) But there was no voice, nor any that answered. And they leaped upon the altar which was made. And it came to pass at noon that Elijah mocked them.

Elijah (D) Cry aloud: for he is a god; either he is talking, or he is pursuing, or he is in a journey, or peradventure he sleepeth, and must be awakened.

Narrator 1 (G) And they cried aloud, and cut themselves with knives and lancets, till the blood gushed out upon them.

Narrator 2 (H) And it came to pass, when midday was past, and they prophesied until the time of the offering of the evening sacrifice, that there was neither voice, nor any to answer, nor any that regarded.

Elijah (D) Come near unto me.

Narrator 1 (G) All the people came near unto him. And he repaired the altar of the Lord that was broken down. And Elijah took twelve stones, according to the number of the tribes of the sons of Jacob, and with the stones he built an altar in the name of the Lord: and he made a trench about the altar as great as would contain two measures of seed. And he put the wood in order, and cut the bullock in pieces, and laid him on the wood.

Elijah Fill four barrels with water, and pour it on the burnt sacrifice and on the wood. Do it the second time.

Narrator 2 And they did it the second time.

Elijah 

Do it the third time.

Narrator 1 And they did it the third time. And the water ran round about the altar and filled the trench.

Narrator 2 It came to pass at the time of the offering of the evening sacrifice that Elijah prayed.

Elijah Lord God of Abraham, Isaac, and of Israel, let it be known this day that thou art God in Israel, and that I am thy servant, and that I have done all these things at thy word. Hear me, O Lord, hear me, that this people may know that thou art the Lord God, and that thou hast turned their heart back again.

Narrator 1 Then the fire of the Lord fell, and consumed the burnt sacrifice, and the wood, and the stones, and the dust, and licked up the water that was in the trench.

People The Lord, he is the God.
The Lord, he is the God.

Elijah Take the prophets of Baal; let not one of them escape.

Narrator 2 And they took them; and Elijah brought them down to the brook Kishon, and slew them there.

Elijah Ahab, Get thee up, eat and drink; for there is a sound of abundance of rain.

Narrator 1 So Ahab went up to eat and to drink.

Narrator 2 (H) Elijah went to the top of Carmel; and he cast himself down upon the earth and put his face between his knees, and said to his servant . . .

Elijah (D) Go up now, look toward the sea.

Servant (E) There is nothing.

Elijah (D) Go again seven times.

Narrator 1 (G) And it came to pass at the seventh time,

Servant (E) Behold, there ariseth a little cloud out of the sea, like a man's hand.

Elijah (D) Go up, say unto Ahab, Prepare thy chariot, and get thee down, that the rain stop thee not.

Narrator 2 (H) It came to pass in the meanwhile, that the heaven was black with clouds and wind, and there was a great rain.

Dealing with Impossible Odds

The Book of Job

Stage Layout*

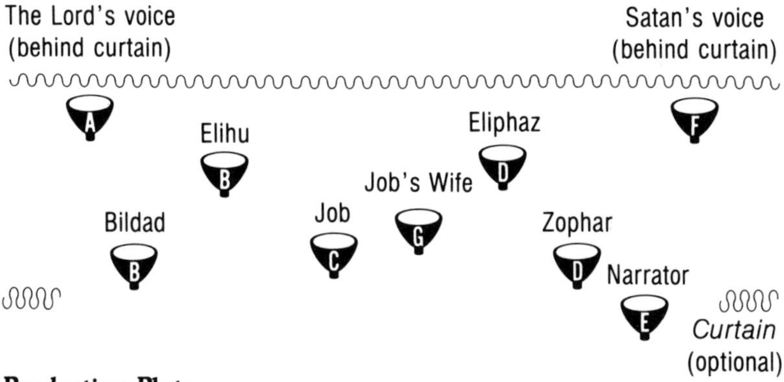

The Lord's voice
(behind curtain)

Satan's voice
(behind curtain)

A

Elihu
B

Eliphaz
D

F

Job's Wife
G

Bildad
B

Job
C

Zophar
D

Narrator
E

Curtain
(optional)

Production Plots

	Lights	Character	Costume	Props
A	White light	The Lord	—	—
B	Green light	Bildad	Green robe	18-inch stool
B	Green light	Elihu	Red robe	30-inch stool
C	Straw light	Job	Black robe	24-inch ladder
D	Purple light	Eliphaz	Purple robe	30-inch stool
D	Purple light	Zophar	Blue robe	18-inch stool
E	Pink light	Narrator	White robe	18-inch stool
F	Red light	Satan	—	—
G	Blue light	Job's Wife	White robe	18-inch stool

*For Production Notes, see page 9.

The Book of Job

Narrator

There was a man in the land of Uz, whose name was Job; and that man was perfect and upright, and one that feared God, and eschewed evil. And there were born unto him seven sons and three daughters. His substance also was seven thousand sheep, and three thousand camels, and five hundred yoke of oxen, and five hundred she asses, and a very great household; so that this man was the greatest of all the men of the east. And his sons went and feasted in their houses, every one his day; and sent and called for their three sisters to eat and drink with them. And it was so, when the days of their feasting were gone about, that Job sent and sanctified them, and rose up early in the morning, and offered burnt offerings according to the number of them all.

Job

It may be that my sons have sinned, and cursed God in their hearts.

Narrator

Now there was a day when the sons of God came to present themselves before the Lord, and Satan came also among them. And the Lord said unto Satan—

Lord

Whence comest thou?

Satan

From going to and fro in the earth, and from walking up and down in it.

Lord

Hast thou considered my servant Job, that there is none like him in the earth, a perfect and upright man, one that feareth God, and escheweth evil?

Satan Doth Job fear God for nought? Hast thou not made an hedge about him, and about his house, and about all that he hath? thou hast blessed the work of his hands, and his substance is increased in the land. But put forth thine hand now, and touch all that he hath, and he will curse thee to thy face.

Lord Behold, all that he hath is in thy power; only upon himself put not forth thine hand.

Narrator So Satan went forth from the presence of the Lord. And there was a day when his sons and daughters were eating and drinking wine in their eldest brother's house: and there came a messenger unto Job.

Messenger 1
Bildad

The oxen were plowing, and the asses feeding beside them: and the Sabeans fell upon them, and took them away; yea, they have slain the servants with the edge of the sword; and I only am escaped alone to tell thee.

Narrator While he was yet speaking, there came also another.

Messenger 2
Zophar

The fire of God is fallen from heaven, and hath burned up the sheep, and the servants, and consumed them; and I only am escaped alone to tell thee.

Narrator 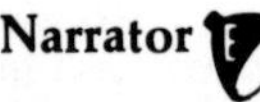 While he was yet speaking, there came also another.

Messenger 3
Elihu

The Chaldeans made out three bands, and fell upon the camels, and have carried them away, yea, and slain the servants with the edge of the sword; and I only am escaped alone to tell thee.

Narrator While he was yet speaking, there came also another;

Messenger 4
Eliphaz

Thy sons and thy daughters were eating and drinking wine in their eldest brother's house; and, behold, there came a great wind from the wilderness, and smote the four corners of the house, and it fell upon the young men, and they are dead; and I only am escaped alone to tell thee.

Narrator Job arose, and rent his mantle, and shaved his head, and fell down upon the ground, and worshipped.

Job Naked came I out of my mother's womb, and naked shall I return thither: the Lord gave, and the Lord hath taken away; blessed be the name of the Lord.

Narrator In all this Job sinned not, nor charged God foolishly. Again there was a day when the sons of God came to present themselves before the Lord, and Satan came also among them to present himself before the Lord.

Lord From whence comest thou?

Satan From going to and fro in the earth, and from walking up and down in it.

Lord Hast thou considered my servant Job, that there is none like him in the earth, a perfect and an upright man, one that feareth God, and escheweth evil? and still he holdeth fast his integrity, although thou movedst me against him, to destroy him without cause.

Satan Skin for skin, yea, all that a man hath will he give for his life. But put forth thine hand now, and touch his bone and his flesh, and he will curse thee to thy face.

Lord Behold, he is in thine hand; but save his life.

Narrator So Satan went forth from the presence of the Lord, and smote Job with sore boils from the sole of his foot unto his crown. And he took him a potsherd to scrape himself withal; and he sat down among the ashes.

Job's wife Dost thou still retain thine integrity? curse God, and die!

Job Thou speakest as one of the foolish women speaketh. What? shall we receive good at the hand of God, and shall we not receive evil?

Narrator Now when Job's three friends heard of all this evil that was come upon him, they came every one from his own

place: Eliphaz the Temanite, and Bildad the Shuhite, and Zophar the Naamathite: for they had made an appointment together to come to mourn with him and to comfort him. And when they lifted up their eyes afar off, and knew him not, they lifted up their voice and wept; and they rent every one his mantle, and sprinkled dust upon their heads toward heaven. So they sat down with him upon the ground seven days and seven nights, and none spake a word unto him: for they saw that his grief was very great. After this opened Job his mouth, and cursed his day.

Job

Let the day perish wherein I was born, and the night in which it was said, There is a man child conceived. Let that day be darkness; let not God regard it from above, neither let the light shine upon it. Let darkness and the shadow of death stain it; let a cloud dwell upon it; let the blackness of the day terrify it. For now should I have lain still and been quiet, I should have slept: then had I been at rest. There the wicked cease from troubling; and there the weary be at rest.

Why is light given to a man whose way is hid, and whom God hath hedged in?

For the thing which I greatly feared is come upon me. I was not in safety, neither had I rest, neither was I quiet; yet trouble came.

Narrator Then Eliphaz answered and said . . .

Eliphaz If we assay to commune with thee, wilt thou be grieved? but who can withhold himself from speaking? Behold, thou hast instructed many, and thou hast strengthened the weak hands. Thy words have upholden him that was falling, and thou hast strengthened the feeble knees.

But now it is come upon thee, and thou faintest; it toucheth thee, and thou art troubled. Is not this thy fear, thy confidence, thy hope, and the uprightness of thy ways? Remember, I pray thee, who ever perished, being innocent? or where were the righteous cut off?

Behold, happy is the man whom the Lord correcteth: therefore despise not thou the chastening of the Almighty: For he maketh sore, and bindeth up: he woundeth, and his hands make whole. He shall deliver thee in six troubles: yea, in seven there shall no evil touch thee. Thou shalt know that thy tabernacle shall be in peace; and thou shalt visit thy habitation, and shalt not sin. Thou shalt know also that thy seed shall be great, and thine offspring as the grass of the earth. Thou shalt come to thy grave in a full age, like as a shock of corn cometh in in his season. Lo this, we have searched it, so it is; hear it, and know thou it for thy good.

Job

Oh that my grief were thoroughly weighed and my calamity laid in the balances together! What is my strength, that I should hope? and what is mine end, that I should prolong my life?

Is there not an appointed time to man upon earth? When I lie down, I say, When shall I arise, and the night be gone? My flesh is clothed with worms and clods of dust; my skin is broken, and become loathsome.

How long wilt thou not depart from me, nor let me alone! I have sinned; what shall I do unto thee, O thou preserver of men? why hast thou set me as a mark against thee, so that I am a burden to myself? And why dost thou not pardon my transgression, and take away mine iniquity? for now shall I sleep in the dust; and thou shalt seek me in the morning, but I shall not be.

Bildad

How long wilt thou speak these things? and how long shall the words of thy mouth be like a strong wind? Doth God pervert judgment? or doth the Almighty pervert justice? If thou wert pure and upright; surely now he would awake for thee, and make the habitation of thy righteousness prosperous. Though thy beginning was small, yet thy latter end should greatly increase.

Behold, God will not cast away a perfect man, neither will he help the evildoers: Till he fill thy mouth with laughing and thy lips with rejoicing. They that hate thee shall be clothed with shame; and the dwelling place of the wicked shall come to nought.

Job

My soul is weary of my life; I will leave my complaint upon myself; I will speak in bitterness of my soul. I will say unto God, do not condemn me; shew me wherefore thou contendest with me.

If I sin, then thou markest me, and thou wilt not acquit me from mine iniquity. If I be wicked, woe unto me; and if I be righteous, yet will I not lift up my head. I am full of confusion; therefore see thou mine affliction; for it increaseth.

Are not my days few? cease then, and let me alone, that I may take comfort a little. But I know that my Redeemer liveth.

Zophar

Should not the multitude of words be answered? and should a man full of talk be justified? Should thy lies make men hold their peace? and when thou mockest, shall no man make thee ashamed? For thou hast said, My doctrine is pure, and I am clean in thine eyes. But oh that God would speak, and open his lips against thee; And that he would shew thee the secrets of wisdom. Know therefore that God exacteth of thee less than thine iniquity deserveth.

Canst thou by searching find out God? canst thou find out the Almighty unto perfection? It is as high as heaven; what canst thou do? deeper than hell; what canst thou know? The measure thereof is longer than the earth, and broader than the sea. If he cut off, and shut up, then who can hinder him? For he knoweth vain men: he seeth wickedness also; will he not then consider it? For vain man would be wise.

If thou prepare thine heart, and stretch out thine hands toward him; If iniquity be in thine hand, put it far away, and let not wickedness dwell in thy tabernacles. For then shalt thou lift up thy face without spot; yea, thou shalt be stedfast, and shalt not fear: Because thou shalt forget thy misery, and remember it as waters that pass away. And thou shalt be secure, because there is hope; and thou shalt take thy rest in safety. Thou shalt lie down, and none shall make thee afraid. But the eyes of the wicked shall fail, and they shall not escape, and their hope shall be as the giving up of the ghost.

Job

No doubt but ye are the people, and wisdom shall die with you. But I have understanding as well as you; I am not inferior to you: yea, who knoweth not such things as these? I am as one mocked of his neighbour, who calleth upon God, and he answereth him: the just upright man is laughed to scorn.

Hear now my reasoning, and hearken to the pleadings of my lips. Will ye speak wickedly for God? and talk deceitfully for him? Will ye accept his person? will ye contend for God? Is it good that he should search you out? He will surely reprove you, if ye do secretly accept persons. Your remembrances are like unto ashes, your bodies to bodies of clay.

Hold your peace, let me alone that I may speak, and let come on me what will. Though he slay me, yet will I trust in him. He also shall be my salvation: for an hypocrite shall not come before him. Hear diligently my speech, and my declaration with your ears. Behold now, I have ordered my cause; I know that I shall be justified. Only do not two things unto me! Make me to know my transgression and my sin. O that thou wouldst hide me in the grave, that thou wouldst keep me secret until thy wrath be past.

Narrator

So these three men (Eliphaz, Bildad, and Zophar) ceased to answer Job, because he was righteous in his own eyes. Then was kindled the wrath of Elihu against Job because he justified himself rather than God. Against his three friends was his wrath kindled, because they had found no answer, and yet had condemned Job.

Now Elihu had waited till Job had spoken, because they were elder than he. When Elihu saw that there was no answer in the mouth of these three men, then his wrath was kindled.

Elihu

I am young, and ye are very old; wherefore I was afraid and durst not shew you mine opinion. I said, Days should speak, and multitude of years should teach wisdom. But there is a spirit in man: and the inspiration of the Almighty giveth them understanding. Great men are not always wise: neither do the aged understand judgment. Yea, I attended to you, and behold, there was none of you that convinced Job or that answered his words. My words shall be of the uprightness of my heart. If thou canst answer me, set thy words in order before me.

Behold, I am according to thy wish in God's stead: I also am formed out of the clay. Behold, my terror shall not make thee afraid. Surely thou hast spoken in mine hearing, and I have heard the voice of thy words, saying, I am clean without transgression, I am innocent; neither is there iniquity in me.

Thinkest thou this to be right, that thou saidst, My righteousness is more than God's. For thou saidst, What advantage will it be unto thee? and, What profit shall I have, if I be cleaned from my sin? I will answer thee, and thy companions with thee. Look unto the heavens, and see; and behold the clouds which are higher than thou. If thou sinnest, what doest thou against him? or if thy transgressions be multiplied, what doest thou unto him? If thou be righteous, what givest thou him? or what receiveth he of thine hand?

Thy wickedness may hurt a man as thou art; and thy righteousness may profit the son of man: By reason of the multitude of oppressions they make the oppressed to cry: they cry out by reason of the arm of the mighty. But none saith, where is God my Maker, who giveth songs in the night; Who teacheth us more than the beasts of the earth, and maketh us wiser than the fowls of heaven?

Surely God will not hear vanity, neither will the Almighty regard it. Hearken unto this, O Job: stand still and consider the wondrous works of God.

And now men see not the bright light which is in the clouds. Fair weather cometh out of the north: with God is terrible majesty. Touching the Almighty, we cannot find him out: he is excellent in power, and in judgment, and in plenty of justice: he will not afflict. Men do therefore fear him: he respecteth not any that are wise of heart.

Narrator Then the Lord answered Job out of the whirlwind . . .

Lord

Who is this that darkeneth counsel by words without knowledge? Gird up thy loins like a man; for I will demand of thee, and answer thou me. Where wast thou when I laid the foundations of the earth? declare, if thou hast understanding. Who hath laid the measures thereof? Whereupon are the foundations thereof fastened? or who laid the cornerstone thereof? Or who shut up the sea with doors? Where is the way where light dwelleth? and as for darkness, where is the place thereof? Hast thou entered into the treasures of the snow? By what way is the light parted? Canst thou lift up thy voice to the clouds, that abundance of waters may cover thee? Who hath put wisdom in the inward parts? or who hath given understanding to the heart? Shall he that contendeth with the Almighty instruct him? he that reproveth God, let him answer it.

Job

Behold, I am vile; what shall I answer thee? I will lay mine hand upon my mouth. Once have I spoken; but I will not answer: yea, twice; but I will proceed no further.

Lord

Gird up thy loins like a man: I will demand of thee, and declare thou unto me. Wilt thou also disannul my judgment? wilt thou condemn me, that thou mayest be righteous? Hast thou an arm like God? Deck thyself now with majesty and excellency; and array thyself with glory and beauty. Cast abroad the rage of thy wrath: and behold everyone that is proud, and bring him low; and tread

down the wicked in their place. Bind their faces in secret. Then will I also confess unto thee that thine own right hand can save thee.

Job

I know that thou canst do everything, and that no thought can be withholden from thee. Therefore have I uttered that I understood not; things too wonderful for me, which I knew not. Hear, I beseech thee, and I will speak: I will demand of thee, and declare thou unto me. I have heard of thee by the hearing of the ear: but now mine eye seeth thee. Wherefore I abhor myself, and repent in dust and ashes.

Narrator

And it was so, that after the Lord had spoken these words unto Job, the Lord said to Eliphaz . . .

Lord

My wrath is kindled against thee, and against thy two friends: for ye have not spoken of me the thing that is right, as my servant Job hath.

Therefore take unto you now seven bullocks and seven rams, and go to my servant Job, and offer up for yourselves a burnt offering; and my servant Job shall pray for you: for him will I accept: lest I deal with you after your folly, in that ye have not spoken of me the thing which is right, like my servant Job.

Narrator

So Eliphaz the Temanite and Bildad the Shuhite and Zophar the Naamathite went, and did as the Lord commanded them: the Lord also accepted Job. And the Lord turned the captivity of Job, when he prayed for his friends: also the Lord gave Job twice as much as he had before. Then came there unto him all his brethren, and all his sisters, and all they that had been of his acquaintance before, and did eat bread with him in his house: and they bemoaned him, and comforted him over all the evil that the Lord had brought upon him: every man also gave him a piece of money, and every one an earring of gold. So the Lord blessed the latter end of Job, more than his beginning.

Walking Together with God

Daniel, Shadrach, Meshach, Abednego

Stage Layout*

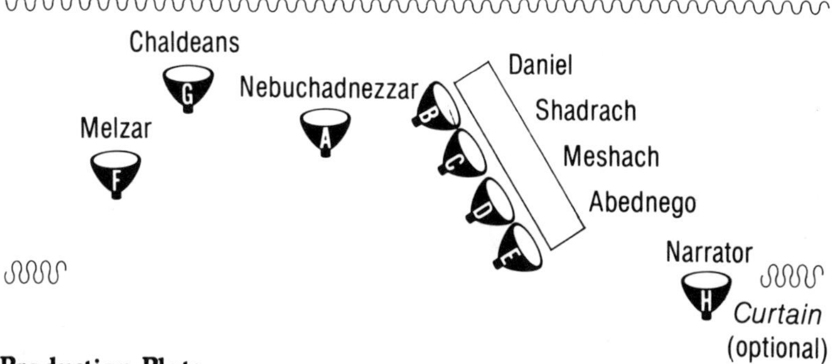

Production Plots

	Lights	Character	Costume	Props
A	Purple light	Nebuchadnezzar	Purple robe	30-inch stool
B	Blue light	Daniel	Blue robe	18-inch bench
C	Yellow light	Shadrach	Brown robe	
D	Red light	Meshach	Brown robe	
E	Straw light	Abednego	Brown robe	
F	Purple light	Prince of Eunuchs Melzar	Black robe	24-inch ladder
G	Blue light	Chaldeans Herald Counsellor	Black robe	24-inch ladder
H	White light	Narrator	White robe	18-inch stool

*For Production Notes, see page 9.

Daniel 1-3

Narrator

When Nebuchadnezzar king of Babylon had come to Jerusalem and besieged the city, he ordered Ashpenaz the master of his eunuchs, saying. . .

Nebuchad-nezzar

Bring certain of the children of Israel, of the king's seed, and of the princes; children in whom is no blemish, but well favoured, and skilful in all wisdom, cunning in knowledge, and understanding science, and such as have ability in them to stand in the king's palace, and whom we might teach the learning and the tongue of the Chaldeans.

Narrator

And the king appointed them a daily provision of the king's meat, and of the wine which he drank: so nourishing them three years, that at the end thereof they might stand before the king.

Now among those were the children of Judah, Daniel, Shadrach, Meshach, and Abednego. But Daniel purposed in his heart that he would not defile himself with the portion of the king's meat, nor with the wine which he drank: therefore he requested of the prince of the eunuchs that he might not defile himself. Now God had brought Daniel into favour and tender love with the prince of the eunuchs.

Prince of the Eunuchs

I fear my lord, the king, who hath appointed your meat and your drink: for why should he see your faces worse liking than the children which are of your sort? then shall ye make me endanger my head to the king.

Narrator

Then said Daniel to Melzar, whom the prince of the eunuchs had set over Daniel, Shadrach, Meshach, and Abednego . . .

Daniel

Prove thy servants, I beseech thee, ten days; and let them give us pulse to eat, and water to drink. Then let our countenances be looked upon before thee, and the countenance of the children that eat of the portion of the king's meat: and as thou seest, deal with thy servants.

Melzar

I will consent to this matter and prove you for the period of ten days.

Narrator

At the end of ten days their countenances appeared fairer and fatter in flesh than all the children which did eat the portion of the king's meat.

Melzar

I will take away the portion of the king's meat, and the wine that they should drink, and give them pulse.

Narrator

As for these four children, God gave them knowledge and skill in all learning and wisdom: and Daniel had understanding in all visions and dreams. Now at the end of the days that the king had said he should bring them in, the prince of the eunuchs brought them in before Nebuchadnezzar. And the king communed with them.

Nebuchad-nezzar

Among them all I find none like Daniel, Meshach, Shadrach, and Abednego as they stand before me. In all matters of wisdom and understanding that I enquire of them, I find them ten times better than all the magicians and astrologers that are in all my realm.

Narrator

And Daniel continued even unto the first year of King Cyrus.

In the second year of the reign of Nebuchadnezzar, the king made an image of gold, whose height was threescore cubits, and the breadth thereof six cubits: he set it up in the plain of Dura, in the province of Babylon. Then Nebuchadnezzar the king sent to gather together the princes, the governors, and the captains, the judges, the treasurers, the counsellors, the sheriffs, and all the rulers of the provinces, to come to the dedication of the image which Nebuchadnezzar the king had set up. And when all were gathered together unto the dedication of the image that Nebuchadnezzar the king had set up, they stood before the image.

Herald

To you it is commanded, O people, nations and languages, that at what time ye hear the sound of the cornet, flute, harp, sackbut, psaltery, dulcimer, and all kinds of musick, ye fall down and worship the golden image that Nebuchadnezzar the king hath set up: Whoso falleth not down and worshippeth shall the same hour be cast into the midst of a burning fiery furnace.

Narrator

At that time when all heard the sound of the cornet, flute, harp, sackbut, psaltery, and all kinds of musick, all the people, the nations and the languages fell down and worshipped the golden image that Nebuchadnezzar the king had set up. At that time certain Chaldeans came near and accused the Jews. They spake to the king Nebuchadnezzar . . .

Chaldeans

O king, live forever. Thou hast made a decree, that every man that shall hear the sound of all kinds of musick shall fall down and worship the golden image; whoso falleth not down and worshippeth, that he should be cast into the midst of a burning fiery furnace. There are certain Jews whom thou hast set over the affairs of the province of Babylon, Shadrach, Meshach, and Abednego; these men, O king, have not regarded thee: they serve not thy gods, nor worship the golden image which thou hast set up.

Narrator

Then Nebuchadnezzar in his rage and fury commanded to bring Shadrach, Meshach, and Abednego. They brought these men before the king.

Nebuchad-nezzar

Is it true, O Shadrach, Meshach, and Abednego, do not ye serve my gods, nor worship the golden image which I have set up? Now if ye be ready that at what time ye hear the sound of all kinds of musick, ye fall down and worship the image which I have made; well: but if ye worship not, ye shall be cast the same hour into the midst of a burning fiery furnace; and who is that God that shall deliver you out of my hands?

Shadrach Meshach Abednego

O, Nebuchadnezzar, we have no need to answer thee in this matter. If it be so, our God whom we serve is able to deliver us from the burning fiery furnace, and he will deliver us out of thine hand, O king. But if not, be it known unto thee, O king, that we will not serve thy gods, nor worship the golden image which thou hast set up.

Narrator H

Then was Nebuchadnezzar full of fury and the form of his visage was changed against Shadrach, Meshach, and Abednego.

Nebuchadnezzar

I command that they should heat the furnace seven times more than it was wont to be heated. Have the most mighty men that are in my army bind Shadrach, Meshach, and Abednego and cast them into the burning fiery furnace.

Narrator H

Then these men were bound in their coats, their hosen, and their hats, and their other garments, and were cast into the midst of the burning fiery furnace. Because the king's commandment was urgent, and the furnace exceeding hot, the flame of the fire slew those men that took up Shadrach, Meshach, and Abednego. And these three men, Shadrach, Meshach, and Abednego, fell down bound into the midst of the burning fiery furnace. Then Nebuchadnezzar was astonied, and rose up in haste, and spake, and said unto his counselors . . .

Nebuchadnezzar

Did not we cast three men bound into the midst of the fire?

Counsellor True, O king.

Nebuchadnezzar Lo, I see four men loose, walking in the midst of the fire, and they have no hurt; and the form of the fourth is like the Son of God.

Narrator Then Nebuchadnezzar came near to the mouth of the burning fiery furnace and spake . . .

Nebuchadnezzar Shadrach, Meshach, and Abednego, ye servants of the most high God, come forth and come hither.

Narrator Then Shadrach, Meshach, and Abednego came forth of the midst of the fire. And the princes, governors, captains, and the king's counsellors, being gathered together, saw these men, upon whose bodies the fire had no power, nor was an hair of their head singed, neither were their coats changed, nor the smell of fire had passed upon them.

Nebuchadnezzar Blessed be the God of Shadrach, Meshach, and Abednego, who has sent his angel and delivered his servants that trusted in him, and have changed the king's word and yielded their bodies that they might not serve nor worship any god, except their own God. Therefore, I make a decree, that every people, nation, and language which speak anything amiss against the God of Shadrach, Meshach, and Abednego shall be cut in pieces, and their houses shall be made a dunghill: because there is no other God that can deliver after this sort.

Narrator Then the king promoted Shadrach, Meshach, and Abednego in the province of Babylon.

Part Two

The New Testament

The Real Christmas Story

Mary, Joseph, Shepherds, and Wise Men

Stage Layout*

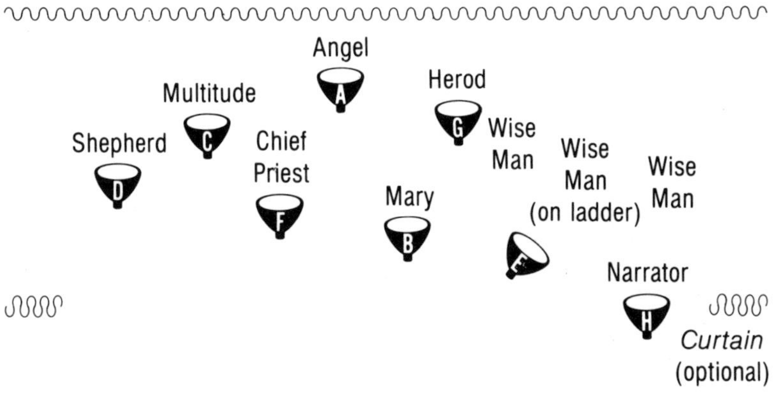

Production Plots

	Lights	Character	Costume	Props
A	White light	Angel	White robe	High ladder (safe)
B	Blue light	Mary	Light blue robe	30-inch stool
C	Red light	Multitude	Brown robe	18-inch stool
D	Straw light	Shepherds	Brown robe	24-inch ladder
E	Yellow light	Wise Men (3)	Gold robe (3)	24-inch ladder
F	Blue light	Chief Priest	Dark blue robe	18-inch stool
G	Purple light	Herod	Purple robe	18-inch stool
H	Pink light	Narrator	Pink robe	18-inch stool

*For Production Notes, see page 9.

Luke 1-2, Matthew 2

Narrator

It came to pass that the angel Gabriel was sent from God unto a city of Galilee, named Nazareth, to a virgin espoused to a man whose name was Joseph, of the house of David; and the virgin's name was Mary. And the angel came unto her . . .

Angel

Hail, thou that art highly favoured, the Lord is with thee: blessed art thou among women.

Fear not, Mary; for thou hast found favour with God. And, behold, thou shalt conceive in thy womb, and bring forth a son, and shalt call his name Jesus. He shall be great, and shall be called the Son of the Highest: and the Lord God shall give unto him the throne of his father David. And he shall reign over the house of Jacob forever; and of his kingdom there shall be no end.

Mary

How shall this be, seeing I know not a man?

Angel

The Holy Ghost shall come upon thee, and the power of the Highest shall overshadow thee: therefore also that holy thing which shall be born of thee shall be called the Son of God.

With God nothing shall be impossible.

Mary

Behold the handmaid of the Lord; be it unto me according to thy word.

My soul doth magnify the Lord and my spirit hath rejoiced in God my Saviour. For he hath regarded the low estate of his handmaiden: for behold, from henceforth all generations shall call me blessed. He that is mighty has done to me great things. Holy is his name.

Narrator

And it came to pass in those days, that there went out a decree from Caesar Augustus, that all the world should be taxed. And all went to be taxed, everyone into his own city. And Joseph also went up from Galilee, out of the city of Nazareth into Judaea, unto the city of David, which is called Bethlehem; (because he was of the house and lineage of David:) to be taxed with Mary his espoused wife, being great with child.

And so it was that, while they were there, the days were accomplished that she should be delivered. And she brought forth her firstborn son, and wrapped him in swaddling clothes, and laid him in a manger; because there was no room for them in the inn.

And there were in the same country shepherds abiding in the field, keeping watch over their flocks by night. And, lo, the angel of the Lord came upon them, and the glory of the Lord shone round about them: and they were sore afraid.

Angel

Fear not: for, behold, I bring you good tidings of great joy, which shall be to all people. For unto you is born this day, in the city of David, a Saviour, which is Christ the Lord. And this shall be a sign unto you; Ye shall find the babe wrapped in swaddling clothes, lying in a manger.

Narrator

And suddenly there was with the angel a multitude of the heavenly host, praising God . . .

Multitude

Glory to God in the highest, and on earth peace, good will toward men.

Narrator

And it came to pass, as the angels were gone away from them into heaven, the shepherds said one to another . . .

Shepherds

Let us now go even unto Bethlehem, and see this thing which is come to pass, which the Lord hath made known unto us.

Narrator And they came with haste, and found Mary, and Joseph, and the babe lying in a manger. And when they had seen it, they made known abroad the saying which was told them concerning this child. The shepherds returned, glorifying and praising God for all the things that they had heard and seen as it was told unto them.

Now when Jesus was born in Bethlehem of Judaea, in the days of Herod the king, behold, there came wise men from the East to Jerusalem.

Wise Men Where is he that is born King of the Jews? for we have seen his star in the East, and are come to worship him.

Narrator When Herod the king heard these things, he was troubled. And when he had gathered all the chief priests and scribes of the people together, he demanded of them where Christ should be born.

Chief Priest In Bethlehem of Judaea: for thus it is written by the prophet, And thou Bethlehem, in the land of Juda, art not the least among the princes of Juda: for out of thee shall come a Governor, that shall rule my people Israel.

Narrator Then Herod privily called the wise men.

Herod What time did the star appear? Go and search diligently for the young child; and when ye have found him, bring me word again, that I may come and worship him also.

Narrator When they had heard the king, they departed: and, lo, the star, which they saw in the east, went before them, till it came and stood over where the young child was. When they saw the star, they rejoiced with exceeding great joy. And when they were come into the house, they saw the young child with Mary his mother, and fell down, and worshipped him:

Wise Man 1 My gift is gold.

Wise Man 2 I present frankincense.

Wise Man 3 I bring thee myrrh.

Narrator Being warned of God in a dream that they should not return to Herod, they departed into their own country another way.

The Joyful Homecoming

The Prodigal Son

Stage Layout*

Servant

C

Father

B

Elder Son

D

Younger Son

A

Narrator

E

Curtain (optional)

Production Plots

	Lights	Character	Costume	Props
A	Red light	Younger Son	Red robe	24-inch ladder
B	Blue light	Father	Blue robe	30-inch stool
C	Straw light	Servant	Black robe	18-inch stool
D	Red light	Elder Son	Brown robe	24-inch ladder
E	Pink light	Narrator	White robe	18-inch stool

*For Production Notes, see page 9.

Luke 15

Narrator

Then drew near unto him all the publicans and sinners for to hear him. A certain man had two sons. And the younger of them said to his father . . .

Younger Son

Father, give me the portion of goods that falleth to me.

Narrator

And he divided unto them his living. And not many days after, the younger son gathered all together, and took his journey unto a far country, and there wasted his substance with riotous living. And when he had spent all, there arose a mighty famine in that land; and he began to be in want. He went and joined himself to a citizen of that country, who sent him into his fields to feed swine. He would have filled his belly with the husks that the swine did eat: and no man gave unto him. And when he came to himself, he said . . .

Younger Son

How many hired servants of my father's have bread enough and to spare, and I perish with hunger! I will arise and go to my father, and will say unto him, Father, I have sinned against heaven and before thee, and am no more worthy to be called thy son: make me as one of thy hired servants.

Narrator

And he arose, and came to his father. When he was yet a great way off, his father saw him, and had compassion, and ran and fell on his neck and kissed him.

Younger Son

Father, I have sinned against heaven and in thy sight, and am no more worthy to be called thy son.

Father

Servants, bring forth the best robe and put it on him; and put a ring on his hand, and shoes on his feet. Bring hither the fatted calf, and kill it, and let us eat and be merry. For this my son was dead, and is alive again; he was lost and is found.

Narrator

And they began to be merry. Now his elder son was in the field: and as he came and drew nigh to the house, he heard musick and dancing. And he called one of the servants, and asked what these things meant.

Servant

Thy brother is come; and thy father hath killed the fatted calf, because he hath received him safe and sound.

Narrator

He was angry and would not go in: therefore came his father out and entreated him.

Elder Son

Lo, these many years do I serve thee, neither transgressed I at any time thy commandment: and yet thou never gavest me a kid, that I might make merry with my friends. But as soon as this thy son was come, which hath devoured thy living with harlots, thou hast killed for him the fatted calf.

Father

Son, thou art ever with me, and all that I have is thine. It was meet that we should make merry, and be glad: for this thy brother was dead, and is alive again; and was lost, and is found.

In Remembrance of Me

The First Communion

Stage Layout*

Jesus' voice
(behind curtain)

A

Peter — C

John — B

Judas — D

High Priest — E

Narrator — F

Curtain
(optional)

Production Plots

	Lights	Character	Costume	Props
A	White light	Jesus	—	—
B	Blue light	John	Blue robe	24-inch ladder
C	Red light	Peter	Brown robe	24-inch ladder
D	Straw light	Judas	Black robe	24-inch ladder
E	Purple light	High Priest	Purple robe	30-inch stool
F	White light	Narrator	White robe	18-inch stool

*For Production Notes, see page 9.

Matthew 26; Luke 22; John 13

Narrator The time of the feast of unleavened bread drew nigh, which is called the passover. Then assembled together the chief priests, and the scribes, and the elders of the people, unto the palace of the high priest, called Caiaphas, and they consulted that they might take Jesus by trickery, and kill him.

High Priest We must kill him, but not on the feast day, lest there be an uproar among the people.

Narrator Then entered Satan into Judas Iscariot, who was one of the twelve disciples. And Judas secretly went his way, and communed with the chief priest and the captains, how he might betray Jesus unto them.

Judas  What will ye give me, and I will deliver him unto you?

Narrator They were glad. And they covenanted with him for thirty pieces of silver. Judas promised, and from that time he sought opportunity to betray him. Now on the first day of the feast of unleavened bread the disciples came to Jesus.

John  Where wilt thou that we prepare for thee to eat the passover?

Jesus  Go into the city, and there shall a man meet you bearing a pitcher of water; follow him into the house where he entereth in. Ye shall say unto the goodman of the house, "The Master saith unto thee, Where is the guestchamber where I shall eat the passover with my disciples?" And he shall shew you a large upper room furnished: there make ready.

Narrator And they went, and found as he had said unto them: and they made ready the passover. And when the evening hour was come, he sat down, and the twelve disciples with him. Jesus, knowing that the Father had given all things into his hands, and that he was come from God, and would go to God, riseth from supper, and laid aside his garments; and took a towel and girded himself. After that he poureth water into a basin, and began to wash the disciples' feet, and to wipe them with the towel wherewith he was girded. Then cometh he to Simon Peter.

Peter Lord, dost thou wash my feet?

Jesus What I do thou knowest not now, but thou shalt know hereafter.

Peter 

Thou shalt never wash my feet.

Jesus If I wash thee not, thou hast no part with me.

Peter 

Lord, not my feet only, but also my hands and my head.

Jesus 

He that is washed needeth only to wash his feet, and is clean every whit. Ye are clean. Know ye what I have done to you? Ye call me Master and Lord: and ye say well; for so I am. If I then, your Lord and Master, have washed your feet; ye also ought to wash one another's feet. For I have given you an example, that ye should do as I have done to you.

Verily, verily, I say unto you, the servant is not greater than his lord; neither he that is sent greater than he that sent him. If ye know these things, happy are ye if ye do them.

Narrator And he sat down and did eat.

Jesus Verily, I say unto you, that one of you shall betray me.

Narrator And they were exceeding sorrowful, and began every one of them to say unto him . . .

Peter and John Lord, is it I? Lord, is it I?

Jesus  He that dippeth his hand with me in the dish, the same shall betray me. The Son of man goeth as it is written of him: but woe unto that man by whom the Son of man is betrayed. It had been good for that man if he had not been born.

Narrator Then Judas, which betrayed him, said . . .

Judas Master, is it I?

Jesus Thou hast said.

Narrator And as they were eating, Jesus took bread and gave thanks, and brake it, and gave it to the disciples, and said . . .

Jesus Take, eat; this is my body, which is given for you; this do in remembrance of me.

Narrator And he took the cup, and gave thanks, and gave it to them.

Jesus Drink ye all of it. For this is my blood of the new testament, which is shed for many, for the remission of sins. But I say unto you, I will not drink henceforth of this fruit of the vine, until that day when I drink it new with you in my Father's kingdom.

Narrator And when they had sung a hymn, they went out into the mount of Olives.

Judge and Jury

Pontius Pilate

Stage Layout*

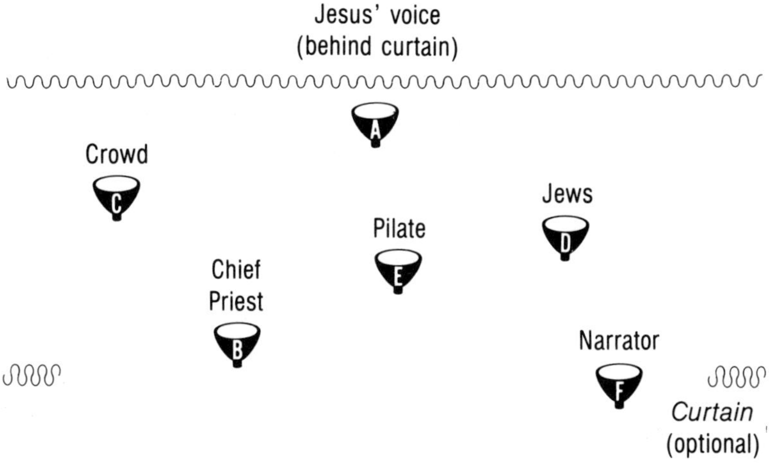

Jesus' voice
(behind curtain)

A

Crowd

C

Jews

Pilate

D

Chief
Priest

E

Narrator

B

F

Curtain
(optional)

Production Plots

	Lights	Character	Costume	Props
A	White light	Jesus	—	—
B	White light	Chief Priest	Black robe	24-inch ladder
C	Red light	Crowd	Brown robe	18-inch stool
D	Pink light	Jews	Brown robe	18-inch stool
E	Purple light	Pilate	Purple robe	30-inch stool
F	White light	Narrator	White robe	18-inch stool

*For Production Notes, see page 9.

John 19

Narrator F	Then Pilate therefore took Jesus, and scourged him. And the soldiers plaited a crown of thorns, and put it on his head, and they put on him a purple robe, and said,
Crowd C	Hail, King of the Jews!
Narrator F	And they smote him with their hands. Pilate went forth and saith unto them,
Pilate E	Behold the man!
Narrator F	When the chief priests and officers saw him, they cried out, saying,
Crowd C	Crucify him, Crucify him.
Pilate E	Take ye him and crucify him; for I find no fault in him.
Jews D	We have a law, and by our law he ought to die, because he made himself the Son of God.
Narrator F	When Pilate therefore heard that saying, he was the more afraid; And went into the judgment hall, and saith unto Jesus,
Pilate E	Whence art thou?
Narrator F	But Jesus gave him no answer.
Pilate E	Speakest thou not unto me? knowest thou not that I have power to crucify thee, and power to release thee?
Jesus A	Thou couldest have no power at all against me, except it were given thee from above: therefore he that delivered me unto thee hath the greater sin.

Narrator And from thenceforth Pilate sought to release him: but the Jews cried out,

Jews If thou let this man go, thou art not Caesar's friend: whosoever maketh himself a king speaketh against Caesar.

Narrator When Pilate heard that saying, he brought Jesus forth, and sat down in the judgment seat in a place that is called the Pavement, but in the Hebrew, Gabbatha. And it was the preparation of the passover, and about the sixth hour: and he said unto the Jews,

Pilate Behold, your King!

Jews Away with him, away with him. Crucify him!

Pilate Shall I crucify your King?

Chief Priest We have no king but Caesar.

Narrator Then delivered he him therefore unto them to be crucified. And they took Jesus, and led him away. And he bearing his cross went forth into a place called the place of a skull, which is called in the Hebrew Golgotha: where they crucified him, and two other with him, on either side one, and Jesus in the midst.

And Pilate wrote a title, and put it on the cross. The writing was *Jesus of Nazareth, the King of the Jews.* This title then read many of the Jews: for the place where Jesus was crucified was nigh to the city: and it was written in Hebrew, and Greek, and Latin. Then said the chief priests of the Jews to Pilate,

Chief Priest Write not, The King of the Jews; but that he said, I am King of the Jews.

Pilate What I have written, I have written.

The Unbelievable Change

The Conversion of Saul

Stage Layout*

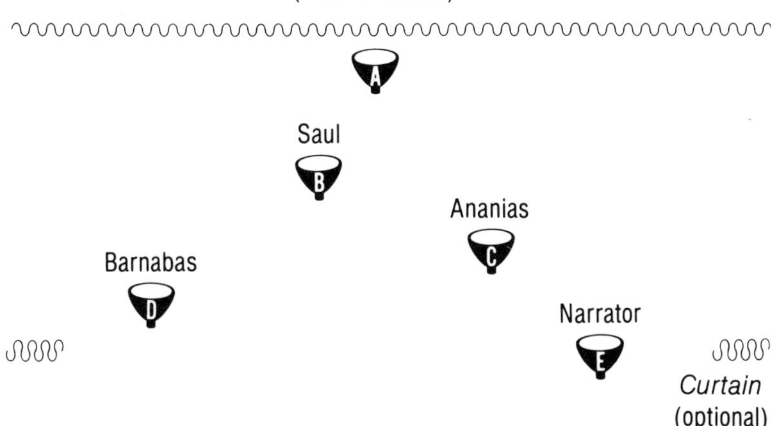

Production Plots

	Lights	Character	Costume	Props
A	White light	Jesus	—	—
B	Straw light	Saul	Brown robe	30-inch stool
C	Blue light	Ananias	Blue robe	24-inch ladder
D	Red light	Barnabas	Brown robe	24-inch ladder
E	Pink light	Narrator	White robe	18-inch stool

*For Production Notes, see page 9.

Acts 9

Narrator 

And Saul, yet breathing out threatenings and slaughter against the disciples of the Lord, went unto the high priest and desired of him letters to Damascus to the synagogues, that if he found any of this way, whether they be men or women, he might bring them bound unto Jerusalem.

And as he journeyed, he came near Damascus: and suddenly there shined round about him a light from heaven: And he fell to the earth, and heard a voice saying unto him . . .

Jesus 

Saul, Saul, why persecutest thou me?

Saul 

Who art thou, Lord?

Jesus 

I am Jesus whom thou persecutest: it is hard for thee to kick against the pricks.

Saul 

(trembling and astonished) Lord, what wilt thou have me to do?

Jesus 

Arise, and go into the city and it shall be told thee what thou must do.

Narrator 

And the men which journeyed with him stood speechless, hearing a voice, but seeing no man. And Saul arose from the earth; and when his eyes were opened, he saw no man: but they led him by the hand, and brought him unto Damascus. He was three days without sight, and neither did eat nor drink. There was a certain disciple at Damascus named Ananias; and to him said the Lord . . .

Jesus 

Ananias.

Ananias Behold, I am here, Lord.

Jesus Arise, go into the street which is called Straight, and inquire in the house of Judas, for one called Saul, of Tarsus: for, behold, he prayeth. He hath seen in a vision a man named Ananias coming in, and putting his hand on him, that he might receive his sight.

Ananias Lord, I have heard by many of this man, how much evil he hath done to thy saints at Jerusalem. Here he hath authority from the chief priests to bind all that call on thy name.

Jesus

Go thy way: for he is a chosen vessel unto me, to bear my name before the Gentiles, and kings and the children of Israel: For I will shew him how great things he must suffer for my name's sake.

Narrator

And Ananias went his way, and entered into the house; and put his hands on him.

Ananias

Brother Saul, the Lord, even Jesus, that appeared unto thee in the way as thou camest, hath sent me, that thou mightest receive thy sight, and be filled with the Holy Ghost.

Narrator

Immediately there fell from his eyes as it had been scales: and he received sight, and arose, and was baptized. When he received meat, he was strengthened. Then was Saul several days with the disciples which were at Damascus.

Straightway he preached Christ in the synagogues, that he is the Son of God. All that heard him were amazed and said . . .

Mob

Is not this he that destroyed them which called on this name in Jerusalem, and came hither for that intent, that he might bring them bound unto the chief priests?

Narrator

But Saul increased the more in strength and confounded the Jews which dwelt in Damascus, proving that this is very Christ.

After many days were fulfilled, the Jews made plans to kill him: but their laying in wait was known of Saul. The

Jews watched the gates day and night to kill him. Then the disciples took him by night, and let him down by the wall in a basket.

When Saul was come to Jerusalem, he wanted to join himself to the disciples: but they were all afraid of him, and believed not that he was a disciple. Barnabas took him and brought him to the apostles.

Barnabas

Brother Saul has seen the Lord in the way. He has spoken to him. Saul has preached boldly at Damascus in the name of Jesus.

Narrator

And he was with them coming in and going out at Jerusalem. Then had the churches rest throughout all Judaea and Galilee and Samaria, and were edified; and walking in the fear of the Lord, and in the comfort of the Holy Ghost, were multiplied.